Praise for

SAIL
INTO YOUR
DREAMS

"Fascinating! This book is like no other—the adventure of the sea interwoven with brilliant information about sailing into your own dreams and bringing them to life. The author has done a wonderful job capturing the excitement of following our bliss. The book is our navigator for living our own lives with integrity, simplicity, and joy. Great reading."

—Hal Zina Bennett,
author of *Write from the Heart* and *Follow Your Bliss*

"*Sail into Your Dreams* allows readers to gently drift through calm seas or navigate through stormy waters to arrive at their own true North. Whether you want to skim the surface or dive in deep, [it] is an indispensable guide book into the uncharted adventure of your life. Immerse yourself in this delightful weave of stories and practical steps to emerge refreshed and on purpose. Don't wait, up-anchor and embark on an unforgettable voyage."

—Diana L. Guerrero,
author of *Blessing of the Animals: A Guide to Prayers & Ceremonies Celebrating Pets & Other Creatures*

About the Author

Karen Mehringer is a psychotherapist with a master's degree in marriage and family therapy, special training in energy transformation, and over ten years of personal development experience. She owns Creative Transformations, where she helps clients fulfill their dreams. After realizing their vision of splitting time between two California dream homes—a mountain cabin and an ocean sailboat—Karen and her husband are off on a new adventure in Colorado. Visit www.liveapurposefullife.com for more information about Creative Transformations.

SAIL
INTO YOUR
DREAMS

8 Steps to Living a
More Purposeful Life

KAREN MEHRINGER

Llewellyn Publications
Woodbury, Minnesota

First Edition
First Printing, 2007

Book design and layout by Joanna Willis
Cover design by Lisa Novak
Cover background image © PhotoDisc
Cover inset photo © Digital Vision

Llewellyn is a registered trademark of Llewellyn Worldwide, Ltd.

Library of Congress Cataloging-in-Publication Data
Mehringer, Karen, 1967–
   Sail into your dreams : 8 steps to living a more purposeful life / Karen Mehringer. 1st ed.
      p. cm.
   Includes bibliographical references
   ISBN-13: 978-0-7387-1053-2
   ISBN-10: 0-7387-1053-9
      1. Self-actualization (Psychology). I. Title

BF637.S4M44 2007
158—dc22   2006052872

Llewellyn Publications
A Division of Llewellyn Worldwide, Ltd.
2143 Wooddale Drive, Dept. 0-7387-1053-9
Woodbury, MN 55125-2989, U.S.A.
www.llewellyn.com

Printed in the United States of America

This book is dedicated to my husband, John,
whose love and support is the wind in my sails,
as I sail into the life of my dreams.

CONTENTS

PART I

DECIDE
TO GO

MY PERSONAL ODYSSEY

If one advances confidently in the direction
of his dreams, and endeavors to live the life
which he has imagined, he will meet with a
success unexpected in common hours.

—HENRY DAVID THOREAU

Surrounded by royal blue water extending beyond the horizon in all directions, no land in sight, I gaze at the path of diamonds dancing on the ocean's surface. The sun radiating on my skin feels like a warm cashmere sweater. It is August 19, 1998, and I am on my first ocean passage of a life-transforming journey, a journey leading to a more authentic and purposeful life.

My journey to living a more purposeful life began in Seattle, Washington, where I lived with my husband, John. Unfulfilled with our lifestyle of working full time, coming home tired, and crashing in front of the TV with little energy left to pursue our passions, our souls cried out, *There must be more to life!*

The work we were doing stifled our creative gifts. While we loved Washington for all of its natural beauty—the green trees, freshwater lakes, and snow-covered mountains—and for the outdoor activities like hiking, camping, and skiing, we found the weather gloomy and rarely engaged in these activities. We wanted to experience life fully, not as bystanders at a football game. So, the decision was made. It was time to set sail for new horizons.

Craving more adventure and fulfillment in our lives, we began taking sailing lessons, an activity we both felt passionate about. Spending time on the ocean enlivened our spirits, causing us to dream and see that there were other possibilities for living. As our interest in sailing grew, we read magazines and books about it. Stories about couples who cruised around the world, slowing down to take time out from their modern lifestyles, inspired us. One book in particular, *Maiden Voyage*, by Tania Aebi, described her adventures at the age of eighteen as the first American woman and youngest person to circumnavigate the world. Discussions ensued. If these people could do it, why couldn't we?

We began looking into options. One was crewing boats. For a minimal amount of money, we could crew on someone else's boat and gain valuable experience while also traveling. As crew, we would share the responsibilities of navigating, helming the boat on scheduled watches, cleaning, and cooking meals. After applying for a couple of positions, we decided on a forty-six-foot sailboat in the process of circumnavigating the world. We would join it on its second leg, cruising from Fiji to Singapore for a six-month period, visiting the countries of Vanuatu, Australia, and Indonesia along the way.

After renting out our house and taking a one-year leave of absence from our employment, we up-anchored and left Seattle on June 1, 1998. Before meeting the boat, we went on a road trip for three weeks, camping out as we explored several different states, looking for a new home—one that resonated more with our souls. Driving east on I-90 through the Cascade Mountains, the sky was bright blue and sunny, the pine needles on the evergreens glistened, and a feeling of summer was in the air. My heart felt lighter and lighter the farther we traveled from the hustle of civilization and our *old* life. Gratitude welled within me for our choice to live adventurously and break out of the confines of our own limiting beliefs about how life *should* be lived. At last, we were free to follow our hearts and begin anew.

Driving through Montana, outside of Yellowstone National Park, I became aware of the majestic beauty of the snow-capped mountains and felt a tremendous connection to the natural surroundings. Reminded of my love for the mountains, I began daydreaming of living in a small cabin closer to nature. Then I thought, *I could never live in the mountains, I love the ocean too much*. Having grown up by the ocean, I could not imagine being landlocked. John felt the same. Our dilemma: could we have both? It was then that the vision was born. We would someday have a cabin in the mountains and a sailboat on the ocean.

Our road trip ended in San Diego, California, where we immediately fell in love with the sunshine, the ocean, and outdoor activities like beach volleyball, boogie boarding, and surfing. The palm trees, warm weather, and laid-back atmosphere induced a feeling of relaxation, like being on vacation. We decided *this* was where we wanted to relocate after returning. Next, we flew to Fiji and met the boat for the next part of our journey.

While living aboard, we had few material possessions, just enough to fit in a large duffle bag. Life became very simple, and we enjoyed being in the moment and slowing down. Dishes were washed by hand, laundry was hung to dry, and meals were a joy to prepare. The only schedule we kept was our watch duty when on offshore passages between destinations. Experiencing how happy we could be with this slower, simpler lifestyle made an impression on us, as did observing the distant cultures we visited. Most people were happy with very little materially. We learned not only about material simplicity, but also about the importance of simplifying our minds. The more we slowed down our thoughts and lessened the distractions in our lives, the more sacred things became and the more present we were to observe and appreciate what was around us. For example, watching the sunset every night was an entertaining ritual that brought us much satisfaction as we observed the colors change from yellow to orange, magenta to red.

After returning to the United States, it took time for us to integrate these lessons. Everything moved so fast. There were too many choices. Just going to the grocery store was enough to make our heads spin, and getting on the freeway felt like being on a roller coaster ride. As we became aware of how materially focused our society was, our resolve to lead a simple life and not buy into the rampant consumer mentality strengthened. But despite our determination, we found ourselves slowly slipping back into the old lifestyle—working just to pay the mortgage, with little energy left to pursue our passions.

My father's untimely death at the age of sixty-four, just nine months after he retired, was the final nudge we needed. It emphasized that we needed to live our dreams—*now*. The time had come to pursue our original vision—a cabin in the mountains and a sailboat on the ocean.

Several weekend visits helped us discover Big Bear, a beautiful mountain resort community in Southern California. One of the advantages of Big Bear over other mountain communities was its proximity to the ocean— only two hours away. We began researching the possibilities. One synchronistic event after another fell into place, showing us that this was where we were supposed to be and that the time was right.

We looked for a cabin with the goal of finding a comfortable place while limiting our monthly expenses so we could afford to buy a sailboat and do work we loved. Freedom and flexibility were our aim. Twice we put offers on homes that were fabulous, but more expensive than our plan. Fortunately, providence stepped in and both offers fell through. Only then did we find the perfect cabin—below our original price range. A year and a half later, we purchased our sailboat, a thirty-foot Catalina, *Windstar*.

Today, I am happier than I have ever felt living in a place. Surrounded by nature, I look out at pine trees, meadows, snow-covered mountains, birds, squirrels, horses, burros, and foxes from the windows of our cabin, and I wake up early in the morning to the sound of coyotes howling instead of commuter traffic. The sun shines nearly every day, and my heart is filled with thankfulness for life.

Having the sailboat as our second home has been tremendously satisfying as well. Long strolls on the beach, watching the sunset, falling asleep to the gentle rocking of the boat and the sound of waves crashing, sailing, and witnessing the sea life—dolphins, whales, seals, and pelicans—are among the things I love.

As a writer, psychotherapist, and the proprietor of Creative Transformations, I work at my own pace, following the rhythms of my body instead of a clock. My thoughts have slowed down, opening space for creativity and passion to bloom. Furthermore, my clients *want* to transform their lives and fulfill their dreams. My work gives me energy instead of draining it. Not only am I living in places I love and doing work I love, but I have energy left to be involved with the community and develop lasting friendships. While manifesting my physical desires, I feel more joy, passion, and purpose in my life. By listening to my heart and making authentic choices, I am living the life of my deepest dreams.

Karen Mehringer
Big Bear City, California
September 2005

INTRODUCTION

EMBARK ON YOUR OWN JOURNEY

Dear reader,

I am honored to share *Sail into Your Dreams: 8 Steps to Living a More Purposeful Life* with you. This book evolved from my own personal awakening and transformation process, which started with the decision to reinvent my life to live more authentically, passionately, and purposefully. By providing you with the tools that helped me, my intention is to empower you to create a more purposeful and satisfying life.

Sail into Your Dreams takes you on your own journey of personal transformation. It incorporates journal entries, stories from my ocean voyage, and my life experiences, as well as those of people I have interviewed, with spiritual wisdom, psychological principles, and practical tools. Like going on an ocean odyssey, it's divided into five parts—"Decide to Go," "Prepare for Your Journey," "Depart for Distant Shores," "The Journey," and "Arrive at Your Destination." The book is about the *process* of sailing into your dreams. The journey begins with waking up and realizing you are dissatisfied with certain aspects of your life, taking full responsibility for your choices thus far, becoming empowered to make different choices, and deciding to embark on a voyage of self-discovery and transformation.

As you prepare for your journey, you will define who you are, what you want, and where you're heading. Understanding you are a magnificent spiritual being with the power to co-create your life while also exploring your unique passions and purpose is integral in discovering who you are and what you truly desire. Now that you know what direction you are heading, you will create room for the life of your dreams by prioritizing your life-force energy, simplifying material possessions, clearing out the clutter, and healing from the past.

Departing for distant shores, it's important to be fully present and engaged. Taking control of the helm and eliminating distractions will allow you to up-anchor, raise the sails, and fully experience what the voyage has to offer. By leaving the safety and comfort of your old life, as you work through limiting beliefs and fears, you will be free to take risks, sail away from the safe harbor, and venture into the unknown.

During the journey, you will swim with the dolphins, creating your own human pod—a community of supportive people. As you develop meaningful relationships, honor one another's uniqueness, and choose to get involved, you will experience a deeper sense of purpose.

Not only will you connect more intimately with others, but also within yourself, with nature, and your Source of wisdom, love, and abundance. Learning tools to tap into your higher guidance, you will be able to navigate the way to your dreams.

Sometimes you'll encounter flat, calm seas, and other times huge, rough seas. But, by seeing the lighthouse in the storm and having trust in a higher purpose, no matter how painful the circumstances, you will be able to overcome adversity. Giving from your heart and being grateful for all of your life experiences and what they've taught you will help you to create deeper meaning.

Detaching from the outcome of your journey and trusting in the process, you will be able to surrender, let go, and enjoy the ride. Accepting where you are in any given moment is like sailing downwind and surfing the waves. Experiencing joy is the purpose of the journey.

When you arrive at your final destination—living a more purposeful life, a life of your deepest dreams and desires—you will realize that there *is* no final destination, that you will continue to evolve and re-create yourself. Therefore, it's all about the process and living your dreams on a daily basis.

Are you living your dreams on a daily basis? Do you feel satisfied with your life? Have you fulfilled your dreams and desires? If not, this book will inspire you to move forward and make positive changes to transform your life. It will also provide you with the practical tools to do so.

As you read *Sail into Your Dreams*, I encourage you to take your time and have a journal and pen nearby so you can process your thoughts, feelings, and experiences. You will gain the most from this book by being an active participant in the process and doing the exercises at the end of each chapter.

Guided meditations and visualizations are offered to assist you in connecting with your inner source of wisdom, love, and joy. You may want to read each meditation through first for its essence and then read it again before closing your eyes and visualizing what is being suggested. For a deeper meditation, record your own voice as you read the words. Speak slowly in a calm, soothing manner, and pause frequently. Let go of your expectations of the end result, and show up present. Each time you do the meditation, you will have a different experience, and the more often you do them, the deeper your experiences will be.

As you decide to embark on a journey of personal transformation by reading this book, applying the tools, and engaging in the exercises and meditations, you will feel a deeper sense of purpose. Your spirit will awaken as you take the steps to reinvent your life and follow your heart. Make a commitment to go—today!

If we all live each day from a place of passion, joy, and purpose, not only will we transform our own lives, but we will also impact those around us, creating a ripple effect throughout our communities and the entire world. May this book be an enjoyable sailing experience on a clear, sunny day, with light winds, calm seas, and dolphins playing on the bow of your boat. Blessings on your journey as you sail into your dreams.

BLESSING

Voyage of the Heart

On your voyage of the heart
Let the dreams of your soul take flight
Give them wings, let them soar

Sail the ocean of love
Surf the waves of peace
Allow the winds of joy to fill your sails as you explore

Rest on the island of contentment
The center of stillness
Amidst the ever-changing sea of life

Visit the shores of gratitude
As you sail to the destination of your dreams . . .
A forever unfolding of your soul's light

PART II

PREPARE
FOR YOUR
JOURNEY

STEP 1

PLOT YOUR OWN COURSE

» Be Authentic

I shall be telling this with a sigh
Somewhere ages and ages hence:
Two roads diverged in a wood, and I—
I took the one less traveled by,
And that has made all the difference.

—ROBERT FROST

October 4, 1998. We are sailing north from Cairns to Darwin, Australia, near a stretch of undeveloped land. As we travel farther away from civilization, I am able to go deeper within myself. The waves rolling under the boat speak to my soul. Their messages reveal the truth of who I am and what my purpose is, causing me to feel refreshed, delighted, and at peace. Like a baby in its mother's womb, I'm being carried and gently nurtured by the ocean while my spirit awakens.

Hear Your Own Voice

The first step to living a purposeful life is to hear your own voice. From the time we were babies, we were given scripts on how to live. Our families instilled beliefs and values in us, society told us what roles to play, and the media showed us how we should look and what we should own. Few of us were encouraged to follow the true desires of our hearts. Often, our hearts contradicted our character's role in the play.

If you want to live a purposeful life and fulfill your dreams, you must throw away these scripts, plot your own course in life, and discern whose voice you are listening to. Is it your own authentic voice, or that of another, imposing his or her values and ideas onto you? The voices of society, the media, and our family and friends are strong, often tugging at us to do the *right thing*. But if the *right thing* isn't true to who we are and what our purpose is, we will be miserable.

How do we know our truth? When we follow our bliss and feel good inside, we are living our truth. Our bodies are remarkable communicators, as they tell us when we are living out of alignment with who we are. If we are unhappy and stressed about work, we may experience headaches or stomachaches. The other day, I felt tension in my forehead, neck, and shoulders, and during meditation, I asked my body what it was trying to communicate. The answer? I had overcommitted myself and was feeling overwhelmed. I had allowed someone to talk me into doing something that wasn't in my best interest, and my body was telling me *no*.

Signs to look for that indicate you may be out of alignment with your truth are anxiety, anger, guilt, despair, dissatisfaction, or physical discomfort or illness. If you are not feeling joy in your life circumstances, whether it's with a job, relationship, or your lifestyle, then it may be time to go within and listen. Are you following your heart and being true to yourself and what you desire? Or are you living a scripted life, doing what you think you *should* be doing?

To hear your own voice, it is helpful to know who you are as an infinite spiritual being, as well as who you are as a special human being with unique gifts and passions. It is also good to know what you want from deep within your heart, aside from family and societal expectations. Learning to maintain your personal power and not allow others' judgments to sway you from your truth is an important step in the process.

By consciously taking the time to slow down and connect deeply within yourself, to listen to your own voice, you will be able to plot an authentic course to a more fulfilling and purposeful life and will experience great joy in the process.

Know Who You Are

The first key to being authentic and creating a life you love is to awaken and remember who you are as a magnificent *spiritual* being connected to all of life, as well as who you are as a unique *physical* being with special talents, gifts, and passions. Here is an example. Imagine for a moment you are standing near the ocean on a beach. Feel the wind gently caressing your skin and the soft, warm sand under your feet. Hear the ocean waves pounding on the shore. Now, picture your life being like one of those waves: as they travel a long distance before crashing on land and being drawn back into the ocean, you travel the distance of life, culminating with the crash—death—and recede back to where you came from—Source.

Now, continue to imagine standing on the shore, and observe the waves as they roll in and break. You'll notice each wave is unique. None are the same; they all have different sizes and shapes, just as our individual lives are unique and have a special purpose. But, despite our uniqueness, we are *always* connected to our Source, like the waves are to the ocean, and are thus part of something much larger than ourselves. Through this connection, we have access to abundant resources and infinite possibilities—to the same vital energy that created us. We are therefore co-creators of our lives and have the power, choice, and freedom to participate in the creation process. It is up to us.

When we awaken and remember who we are as infinite spiritual beings made from divine love and light, we step into our power as co-creators with God and are able to tap into the energy source of creation to attract what we desire into our lives. This energy is often called the un-manifest, the void, or the source of infinite possibilities. In *The Power of Intention*, Dr. Wayne Dyer calls it *intention*. He describes it as a high-frequency energy vibration that is all around us. When we step into our power and are connected to our Source, we attempt to match our energy vibration with the vibration of intention. From this place, it is possible to manifest instantaneously. The following story is an example.

While in the flow with my writing one night, the wind was blowing outside as clouds passed in front of a full moon, leaving a residue of yellow, orange, and purple. I thought, *Wouldn't it be cool to see a rainbow around the moon?* About ten minutes later, I went outside and witnessed a miracle—a complete rainbow circling the moon. Awestruck and filled with gratitude, I began to cry. This experience showed me how quickly we can manifest with our thoughts, especially when we are connected to Source and are in the energy vibrations of love and joy. I also took this as a sign that the project I was working on was in alignment with my highest good. Spirit was confirming I was on track.

When we remember who we are as magnificent, powerful, spiritual beings always connected to Source, and as unique human beings, the world opens up to us, and we realize there are infinite possibilities for creating a purposeful life filled with our deepest dreams and desires. The challenge is to stay in this place of remembrance and to live in our essence on a daily basis. One way to do this is to create an affirmation or mantra you say to yourself daily during prayer or meditation or while taking a shower. An example is, "I am pure divine radiance overflowing with love, light, and joy." As you say this to yourself, create a visual picture of radiant light pouring from you, reaching far out into the galaxy. Feel your power and own it. This is the truth of who you are!

Express Your Passions

Coming into the fullness of our being, of our potential, requires that we know who we are as magnificent spiritual beings while we express our uniqueness through our passions—what it is we love, what makes our heart sing, and what causes us to feel we are touching God. It is different for everyone. Our passions, when combined with our gifts and talents, often lead to our unique purpose or calling. Our deepest dreams and desires also give us clues as to what will fulfill us, feed our spirits, and make a positive difference in the world.

Ideally, our passions will be integrated with our life's work. But expressing our passions is not necessarily what we do for a job to make money. It is how we *are* in the world. For example, maybe you creatively express yourself through writing, drawing, singing, or playing the drums. Maybe you enjoy assisting others in their healing process and naturally gravitate to situations in which you have the opportunity to be of assistance, despite whether you make an income or not. These avenues of expression cause us to feel awake and alive. They reflect who we are as unique individuals.

As we allow our passions to be expressed, we become like instruments, vibrating beautiful music. Spirit is able to work through us, guiding our steps, showing us the tone, tempo, and keys to our music. The details of how to navigate the way to our dreams reveal themselves. We can then step effortlessly into them, sailing smoothly with calm seas, sunny skies, and fair winds. The process takes us where we want to be.

Figuring out who we are regarding our passions and gifts is another process. Often, we do things we don't enjoy as a way of ruling out what *it* is not. But eventually, these experiences give us clues as to what *it* is. For example, while working in advertising sales, I really enjoyed connecting with my clients, working independently, and developing ads—the creative part—but I didn't like the pressure of deadlines and cold calling. I also felt something was missing, as I wanted to make more of a direct difference in people's lives. This experience helped me realize my desire to be a therapist and work independently while creatively expressing myself. Thus, starting my own business was the perfect outlet for my passions and talents.

Susie, a thirty-five-year-old owner of an organic health-food store, was a schoolteacher for twelve years before opening her own business. She enjoyed teaching but always felt restless, which caused her to search for something else. "As a teacher, I felt a real sense of frustration, like I was caged in and suffocating. My creativity wanted to bubble out," she shared.

A previous experience working at a winery in Chile showed her how much she loved things that are natural, things from the earth. She also has a passion for helping others become healthier. When combining her passions with her gifts of being organized and determined, opening her store was a natural fit.

"This is *it*. This is where I'm supposed to be," exclaimed Susie. Her restlessness is gone; she is in alignment with her passions and is making a contribution on a daily basis. Not only is she contributing to individuals and the community, she also sees herself as "a pioneer in the twenty-first century." She said, "I'm parting the way for a healthier earth and for our children to be healthy."

After opening her store and living more passionately, Susie smiled and said, "My life has just started. I'm so much happier and feel like I'm a different person. I have my health back, my mind back, and my sanity back. I feel a deep sense of peace and happiness."

In retrospect, she didn't even realize she wasn't satisfied. "We get good at faking it, convincing ourselves we're okay," she explained.

When asked what the process was for finding what she loves, she stated, "You have to love yourself first and know who you are and where you're coming from. This involves shedding judgments and abusive behaviors, as well as connecting with Source. When we love and forgive ourselves, doors start to open. Spirit says, 'Here's what you're ready to do.'"

Doors began opening early on for Marguerite, a yoga instructor. She is one of those rare people who discovered her passion at a young age, when she began taking yoga classes at thirteen. Teaching now for over sixteen years, she feels like her work is a win-win situation, since she gets paid to do what she loves. "It's a joy. I feel inspired to get up in the morning," shared Marguerite.

An important aspect of her work is that it reinforces her values of engendering peace and health. She is able to make a contribution by assisting others to experience more peace and health, and at the same time, she experiences it for herself. In the past, when working for someone else in a *job*, she would come home tired, feeling as though she were "chained to a cement block going to the bottom of a pool."

Since being in alignment with her passion, Marguerite is more satisfied—"I'm smiling instead of whining, enjoying instead of complaining. Life is much more fulfilling, and I can't wait to get up in the morning."

When we follow our hearts and express our passions in every area of our lives, we give others permission to do the same. Our joy and contentment spill over, creating a ripple effect—like a rock tossed in a lake whose waves reach the other shore, our energy and vibrancy are far-reaching.

Know What You Want

If you find yourself dreading getting up in the morning or frequently feeling drained and tired, maybe you are not living authentically, in alignment with your passions. Maybe you have not found what *it* is yet. The following activities are helpful tools for gaining more clarity and discovering *it*:

- Get a journal out and begin writing about what your unique gifts and talents are. What are you good at that you enjoy doing?

- Write about when you feel passionate. What are you doing when passion is upon you?

- What makes your heart sing? Make a list of a hundred things (people, places, experiences, and so on) that you love. For example: watching the sunset, sleeping under the stars, the color purple, thunder and lightning storms, hot fudge sundaes.

- List twenty-five things you want to experience, do, have, or be that are truly important for you before you die. Name specific activities or events. For example, *travel* is not as clear as *trek the Himalayas for three weeks*.

- Review adult education or extension classes in a catalog, circle the classes that interest you, and begin taking them. Notice if there is a theme to your interests and passions, such as outdoor activities, helping people, artistic expression, or technology.

- Job-shadow or spend time with someone doing what you might want to do. Again, your passions and unique purpose don't have to be *work*-related.

- Research clubs or organizations in your area of interest and ask to participate in a meeting or event. Talk to or interview people you meet. For example, if you are interested in becoming a psychotherapist, research national associations for psychotherapists and find out where a local chapter meeting is being held. Attend the meeting and network. Don't be afraid to reach out to people in your area of interest. What do you have to lose?

- Pray, meditate, and journal for resources, guidance, and clarity on a daily basis. Ask Spirit to show you where to go and who to talk to. Expect resources to show up, and pay attention so you don't miss out on opportunities that come your way.

- Read books and magazines about subjects you feel passionate about.

- Hire a life coach who can help you clarify your dreams and assist you in establishing realistic goals. For more information on life coaching or to find a coach to meet your specific needs, check out the International Coach Federation website: www.coachfederation.org.

- Participate in group workshops or retreats, as others often reflect what we need to see about ourselves.

If you still have trouble knowing what your passions are, then consider how you wish to experience life. For example, do you desire more joy, freedom, peace, or love in your life? Maybe you are lonely and want to feel more connected. Maybe you wish to be more creative or experience more abundance. Spend time journaling for several days and see what emerges. Start the page with, "What I want most in my life is . . ." Set a timer and write nonstop for twenty minutes. Write from your heart, allowing the words to flow, and don't edit what comes out. Even if your dreams seem impossible, they may be the seeds of your true destiny.

Once you have an idea of what you desire, let your intentions be known by creating a detailed vision. Write it down through journaling or making a list; give it creative expression by developing a collage or piece of artwork; visualize it as if it has already manifested in your life; verbalize your vision with a trusted friend; and create a vision notebook or binder to use for dreaming and developing an action plan of how you're going to accomplish that vision. Setting specific intentions engages the power of your mind to work for you in surprising and miraculous ways. It also allows the Universe to work on your behalf.

Here are some examples. About two months before meeting my husband, I created a detailed list of sixty-four qualities I wanted in a partner. On the back, I included a twenty-item list of how I wanted to feel in the relationship, like loved, respected, honored, and accepted for who I am. Looking back on this list, my husband matches every one of the qualities, and I experience feeling just as I intended. Before purchasing our sailboat, we placed a picture of our ideal boat on the refrigerator and decorated a bedroom in our cabin with a sailboat theme. Sure enough, the boat we purchased looked almost identical to the picture hanging on our refrigerator.

When setting your intentions, be patient and flexible, as sometimes things don't go exactly as planned, but may turn out even better. We can't always see the higher picture.

The following is an example of a visualization you can use during meditation to draw what you desire into your life:

Sit comfortably in a chair or cross-legged on a cushion on the floor with your back upright and your hands resting on your lap. Begin by bringing your focus of awareness inside to the core of your being. Notice your breath and allow it to deepen with each inhalation. Create a rhythmic flow by equally spacing your in-breath and out-breath. As you begin to relax, notice any areas in your body that feel tense or uncomfortable, and send breath to them, allowing the tension to soften and release. Next, notice the quality of your thoughts. Attempt to still your mind as you sit peacefully in silent awareness.

From a peaceful, centered place, ask yourself, "What are my deepest dreams and desires?" Pause and notice what emerges. Take several minutes to watch what shows up in your mind's eye. Watch without judgment. Allow your vision to unfold with detail, color, life, and feeling. If more than one vision or desire appears, select the one or the combination that makes you feel most alive. If none appear, then ask how you wish to experience life. Maybe you wish to feel more connected or experience more passion. What would that look like?

Feel the essence of your vision as if it has already happened. Picture yourself feeling vitally alive, and experience the love, joy, and abundance of this reality.

Focus your attention on your heart center and visualize the energy of love pouring out toward your vision, completely saturating it. (You may see it as a color.) This energy is like a magnet, drawing your vision back to you, back inside your heart. As you fill your heart with this loving, abundant energy, imagine it spreading to the rest of your body, to every *organ and cell. Breathe deeply and express gratitude, knowing that your highest good is on its way to you right now.*

When you feel complete, slowly and gently bring yourself back to the room. Pay attention to your breath, and gently open your eyes. Take time to journal about your experience.

Maintain Your Personal Power

When we are in alignment with our truth, living authentically and passionately, we are mirrors for others. Oftentimes, this is threatening for them, because we reflect where they are out of alignment with their soul's purpose. This may cause judgment and criticism. It's important to realize it isn't about us and not take it personally.

Their reactions may also be coming from a place of fear. For example, when John and I moved to the mountains, we had one part-time income between us—my job. He had left a high-paying career in the high-tech industry without a concrete direction for his work, acting on complete faith. This, of course, is contrary to cultural messages about the importance of stability and security and the man being the provider. My husband fought feelings of guilt. He felt subtle pressure from friends and family as their fears came out in the form of questions about what he was going to do for work. Ultimately, he was able to let go of the guilt and pressure, realizing it wasn't personal and about him, but rather about the discomfort and fears others felt when we broke out of the box to follow our hearts.

When we allow others' judgments and criticism to affect us, or advice and opinions to sway us from our truth, we give away our power. For example, I recently found myself feeling anxious. It manifested physically in the form of being tired, distracted, and creatively stuck. As I wrote in my journal and meditated, I realized my power was being drained like a battery slowly dying. I had given it away to a friend whose advice I valued. She had recommended I work on a different writing project than the one I was currently working on. While attempting to sit with the other project for several weeks, nothing came to me. Once I realized what had happened and recommitted myself to the original project, my anxiety melted away and was replaced with passion. My friend's intentions were good, but her advice wasn't in alignment with my truth.

One of the reasons we give our power away is that we desire to please others in order to make them happy and be accepted by them. This pattern is especially evident in women, as we are socialized to be nurturers and put others' needs before our own. If done habitually, our life-force energy is drained, our passions are deadened, and our purpose and dreams go unfulfilled. Whether it's with your partner, kids, pets, friends, family, or neighbors, honor yourself by setting firm boundaries and sticking to them. Ultimately, when we are taking care of ourselves, others respect us and are happier for it as well. For example, if you are feeling burned out and need personal time alone, be clear with your family about your needs and desires. Take a day to yourself to follow your heart and do something you love, or lock yourself in the bathroom with a Do Not Disturb sign on the door and take a warm, luxurious bath. If others attempt to encroach on your space, then firmly but lovingly say no. As a result, you will have more energy to be fully present with your family and friends when you do spend time with them.

Where in your life are you giving away your power? Are you following advice that isn't true to who you are? Are you letting someone else's judgment bother you and affect your decisions? Or are you allowing others to control you and cross your boundaries? Taking back your power may involve speaking honestly with the person who is giving you advice, criticizing you, or trying to manipulate you. Other methods include writing down or saying out loud positive statements about your truth. Or you might just need to take action, like I did, when I recommitted to my writing project. At times, it can be difficult to decide when it's worth our life-force energy to stand up for ourselves or just let something go, so listen to your intuition and always follow your truth.

When we choose to live authentically and passionately, plotting our *own* course to a purposeful life, our mental, emotional, and physical health improves, our outlook becomes more positive, and we are filled with joy, knowing we are in alignment with who we are.

Exercises

1. Sit down, close your eyes, take a few deep breaths, and listen to your body. If you experience tension or discomfort, ask, "Is there a lesson? Am I out of alignment with my truth? What do I need to do differently?" Sometimes the answers are forthcoming: you may see them in a vision, hear them while meditating, or receive clarity through journaling. Other times you need to be patient, allowing them to unfold.

2. Create a mandala of how you see yourself as a magnificent spiritual being. Draw a large circle on a piece of white construction or butcher paper. Within the circle, paint, draw, or color an image representing yourself as a powerful, light-filled being. Place it where you can see it daily.

3. Describe what you would do with your life if you had six months to live. (Money isn't an issue, and you will have perfect health until the end.) Is there anything in your life you would regret if you were to die tomorrow, anything left undone? Explain.

4. Create a "vision binder" for your life. List five to seven areas of importance separately at the top of a blank piece of paper, such as "Relationships," "Career," "Health," "Finances," and so on. (You can separate them with tabs.) Write in detail what your visions are for each area. Allow yourself to dream big and think outside the box. The universe knows no limits! Make sure to date your entries and update the binder at least once a year.

5. Write nonstop for ten minutes about what robs you of your joy and passion. How do you give your power away? Explain. Create a positive affirmation stating your truth, and say it out loud after writing it on a three-by-five-inch index card. Then, place the card where you can see it. Read your affirmation daily until you feel your joy, passion, and power return.

Guided Meditation

This meditation is designed to assist you in feeling and owning your greatness as a magnificent, powerful, spiritual being and your specialness as a unique human being. (Note: This guided meditation was inspired by Sharon McErlane, author of A Call to Power: The Grandmothers Speak; Finding Balance in a Chaotic World.)

Sit comfortably in a chair or cross-legged on a cushion on the floor with your back upright and your hands resting on your lap. Begin by bringing your focus of awareness inside to the core of your being. Notice your breath and allow it to deepen with each inhalation. Create a rhythmic flow by equally spacing your in-breath and out-breath. As you begin to relax, notice any areas in your body that feel tense or uncomfortable, and send breath to them, allowing the tension to soften and release. Next, notice the quality of your thoughts. Attempt to still your mind as you sit peacefully in silent awareness.

Take a moment to honor and acknowledge who you are as a unique human being with special passions, gifts, and desires. You have a unique purpose that no one else can accomplish. With your combination of gifts, talents, and passions, there is no one else in the world like you, nor will there ever be. You are so very special. Allow yourself to feel the specialness of who you are. You are so very loved.

Now, imagine that you are an infinite spiritual being made from radiant light. Picture your radiance, your essence, pouring out from your feet and shooting deep into the earth, anchoring and grounding you. Take a moment to feel your powerful connection to the earth. This radiant light, which is your being, also expands upward toward the sky. Picture it reaching even farther, to the stars, expanding out into the universe. Its reach knows no limits. You are an enormous vertical column of light expanding down through the earth and up to the heavens. Now imagine power and light also pouring out from your sides, reaching far over the horizon, farther than your eyes can see. It pours out from your chest and back area as well, reaching beyond the horizon into infinity. Radiant light is pouring out from you from six different directions. You are the center of a vast sphere of light, expansive and powerful, without limits. This is the truth of who you are. Take a few moments to experience this expanded state and record it within your being. Allow this knowledge of who you are to permeate every cell of your body. How does it feel? Relax and enjoy this experience.

When you feel complete, slowly and gently bring yourself back to the room and open your eyes. Record your experience and any new insights that occurred to you. Try this meditation when you need to feel empowered.

NAVIGATE THE SEA OF CHANGE

» Create Room

Our life is frittered away by detail . . .
Simplicity, simplicity, simplicity! . . .
Simplicity of life and elevation of purpose.

—HENRY DAVID THOREAU

July 16, 1998. We are anchored off the island of Waya in Fiji. After hiking for two hours, we stumble across a village of about two hundred natives. Living in huts, off the land and sea, in harmony with each other and the earth, they have few material possessions and lead a very simple existence. I am touched by how happy, loving, and spiritual they are, their eyes sparkling and their smiles radiating with love and kindness.

Let Go of the Old

We were born to be creators, to give flight to our passions and create abundantly with our life-force energy. The energy of our creations is then recycled to be renewed again. Like the four seasons—spring, summer, fall, and winter—it's a continuous process. Therefore, it's imperative that we let go of the old to make room for the new. For example, dead branches on a tree need to be trimmed in order for beautiful new life to blossom. We need to trim the dead branches from our lives so we can move forward and experience more joy, peace, and fulfillment.

The dead branches might be in the form of toxic relationships (those that are hurtful or draining), unfulfilling jobs, material objects we no longer use or don't like, clutter in our homes and offices, or emotional baggage from the past. When we hold on to things like clutter, destructive relationships, or dissatisfying jobs, our creative energy becomes stagnant. By releasing what no longer serves our highest good, space is created for new, healthier relationships and positive experiences.

Anytime we create room by letting go of the old, we experience change, and even though it's for a positive outcome, navigating the sea of change can be stressful. For example, when John and I prepared to leave Seattle, we experienced a tremendous amount of anxiety due to the amount of detail our plans involved. Consequently, we held weekly meetings to go over our to-do list and given tasks, such as purchasing health insurance and airline tickets, making car payments, renting storage, securing tenants for our house, and finding a home for our pets.

Change can also induce fear. When we leave the comfort zone of our lives, whether a relationship, job, or home, anxiety kicks in because we don't know what to expect. We fear the unknown. Amidst the excitement of planning our adventure, a big question mark about our future appeared before us. *Where will we live when we return? What kind of work will we do? Will we have enough money? Will we be happy?* At times, fear hit like a tidal wave, causing restless nights of sleep.

Letting go often involves a period of grieving, and sometimes we may even need to let go of things we *love* in order to make room for what we *truly desire*. Saying goodbye to friends and family, tears of sadness rolled down my cheeks, knowing we would probably never live in the same city again. Especially difficult was leaving our pets with a friend—my heart broke many times over thinking about them, missing them. I also grieved moving out of our beloved home, although it was easier once all of our possessions were removed, as it became just a shell.

While preparing to leave, I also evaluated my friendships and decided to let go of those that weren't growing, supportive, and positive. As I let go of what wasn't working, my soul began waking up—passion was more alive than ever. A spiritual fountain of energy and vibrancy turned on inside of me.

In *Saying Yes to Change*, Joan Borysenko wrote, "Saying yes to change is an invitation to faith—not the kind that rests on doctrine—but that which is rooted in trusting our own inner experiences as they unfold." As you navigate the sea of change, trust your inner experiences, follow your passion and joy when making decisions, and acknowledge and work through feelings of fear and sadness. As you do, you will move freely into the next chapter of your life, creating room to receive the abundant gifts waiting for you.

Prioritize Your Life-Force Energy

Our life-force energy is composed of the physical, mental, emotional, and spiritual aspects of our being, working together to fulfill our purpose. During our lifetime, we have a certain amount of life-force energy available to us. Therefore, it's important that we prioritize how we spend it according to who we are, our deepest dreams and desires, what's really important to us—our values—and our higher purpose.

One way to discern whether you are spending your life-force energy for the best possible purpose is to determine how you feel. Do you feel more joy, love, peace, or passion when you invest your energy? Or do you feel depleted—physically, emotionally, and spiritually? For example, when you go to work, do you feel energized by how you invest your time? Are you satisfied at the end of the day? Or do you feel burned out, stressed, and emotionally drained?

Since simplifying my lifestyle, I need less to be happy and I am more content to *be* without feeling the need to fill my free time with busyness or my life with more gadgets and toys. Also, I spend less time worrying about how I look. After years of dying my hair to hide the gray, I took a risk and had my hair cut short to allow my natural hair to grow in. I was tired of spending the time, energy, and money resisting something natural—something authentic. I would rather spend my resources for something positive instead. As it turns out, I like my natural silver hair color. Plus, it's so much easier. I risked going against the societal message that looking youthful is important and that having gray hair is a sign of aging and is negative. As a result, this simple change in my life has freed up life-force energy to invest in other areas that are more important to me. The risk has been well worth it.

While birthing my business, I needed to say no to many social invitations in order to focus my energy and allow my business to grow. My tendency has always been to do too much—have too many irons in the fire, so to speak. When we spread our energy too thin, not only do we get burned out, but we are far less likely to experience success or enjoy what we're doing.

Furthermore, we need to be careful about what we commit to, because by stretching ourselves too thin—unkept promises, unfinished business or projects, being late to appointments, unreturned phone calls, things we'll get to later—our minds are filled with distractions, draining our life-force energy and causing unnecessary stress. Our self-esteem also takes a hit as we feel bad or guilty for not keeping our promises. When making a commitment to another person or yourself, follow through, as this will give you a sense of completion and free up energy to spend on other priorities. Or, if you realize you have overcommitted yourself, graciously back out. For example, if you have accepted a dinner invitation and later realize that you are too tired to go and really enjoy yourself, then tell the person who invited you. Be honest and honor yourself. Initially, the other person may feel disappointed, but ultimately everyone involved will benefit by your honesty and example of self-care.

Take time out to reprioritize how you are spending your life-force energy. First, write down what your values are. For example, you may value spending quality time with family and friends, living a balanced life, being healthy, or making use of your fullest potential at work. Your values are personal and stem from deep within you, so go within and listen. Journal if you need to gain clarity.

Next, make a list of your deepest dreams and desires. Then, ask yourself, "Am I spending my energy in ways that are in alignment with my values and desires? If not, what can I say no to or let go of in order to make more room for living a purposeful life?" For instance, if being healthy is at the top of your values list and you desire more energy but are spending little time taking care of yourself, you will want to find ways to cut back on other, less important priorities to make room for self-care activities such as exercising and preparing healthy foods. In order to make these changes, you will first need to be clear on where you are spending your time, so keep a daily record for a week. Chart your activities and how much time they take. For example, how many hours or minutes do you spend sleeping, eating, dressing, bathing, working, exercising, talking to friends, and so on?

After gaining clarity about your priorities and how you are using your time, begin making small changes by spending your life-force energy on what is really important to you. As you do this, notice how your vitality increases.

Choose Supportive Relationships

One area to examine when choosing where to prioritize your energy is your relationships. It's important to be surrounded by people who support your being 100 percent who you are, and who give you positive energy rather than drain your energy. For example, trees nurture and sustain life just by their essence. They give off oxygen, enabling us to breathe, and provide food and shelter for birds, squirrels, and other animals and insects. Even when dead, a tree is life-sustaining and provides shelter and food. We are like trees in that we have the opportunity to positively affect others around us. But, unlike trees, we can have a negative impact as well—instead of enhancing life around us, our energy can drain it. Endeavoring to live an authentic and purposeful life, we need to consider our relationships. Are they life-enhancing—providing us with oxygen to breathe, such as the trees—or are they draining our life-force energy?

When choosing supportive relationships, sometimes we need to let go of or distance ourselves from unhealthy ones. These relationships, both supportive and unhealthy, include anyone with whom you interact on a regular basis, such as coworkers, friends, family, neighbors, and romantic partners. An example of a draining relationship is when one person talks too much, not allowing space for the other person to speak. Judging, criticizing, blaming, and complaining are also energy-draining behaviors to look out for. Healthy qualities in a relationship are honesty, patience, compassion, acceptance, and understanding. A supportive relationship is mutually beneficial, empowering and uplifting both people involved.

Once you have determined a relationship is unsupportive, figuring out how to move on can be challenging. Writing a letter or expressing your feelings in a face-to-face conversation are the most honest and direct methods. Compassion is important when using this approach, as well as using "I" statements when describing your thoughts and feelings instead of blaming the other person. For example, you might say, "I feel tired and drained when you complain to me about your work," instead of, "You are draining me." This honest approach allows the other person to make changes to rectify the friendship or improve on future relationships. A more subtle approach is to distance yourself gradually by saying no to invitations or calling less frequently. If the relationship is no longer working for you, it may be unhealthy for the other person as well, so you will both benefit from distancing yourself and moving on.

Denise, a single forty-four-year-old who works in catering, moved from San Diego to Big Bear to search for a quieter life. She decided this was the perfect opportunity to evaluate her friendships and pull away from those draining her. She began noticing how she felt around certain people or after getting off the phone with someone. A little at a time, she moved away from the people who "zapped" her energy, saying no to social invitations and distancing herself.

Denise said, "I released people's drama. Friends don't call anymore with drama, and as a result, a huge amount of time and energy has been freed up."

She also shared that the process of moving on from unhealthy relationships can be painful and take time. "You need to be comfortable being alone, because when you move on, there is a void. You have to trust that eventually you will understand why. It doesn't mean the person is bad or you're a bad person, so don't judge or blame them, but they just aren't a healthy fit for you—like clothing, sometimes people don't fit like they used to and you have to let them go."

Denise went on to explain, "Ultimately, when you are doing what's best for you, it's also best for the other person."

Take time to evaluate your relationships. Are there people in your life who are draining your energy? If so, consider the costs of remaining in the relationship versus the benefits of what you gain from continuing your connection. Maybe the other person is temporarily going through a difficult time and as a good friend, the best thing to do is to hang in there with them and support them. If the problem is perpetual, maybe your personalities are incompatible. Or maybe you have simply outgrown the friendship. Whatever the cause, determine if it may be time to let go.

As you sail into the life of your dreams, spend time with people who accept and love you for who you are, people who you feel energized by being around. By choosing supportive relationships, you are preparing a solid foundation for your journey.

Simplify Material Possessions

The more we complicate our lives with *things*, the more distracted we are from what is really important, like maintaining our health, spending quality time with family and friends, expressing ourselves creatively, and making a contribution with our talents. Look at your core values, which you identified in the previous section. What really matters to you? Where do you want to spend your lifeforce energy? When you go to purchase something, ask, "Is this *thing* worth working this many hours to pay for and take care of? Will my enjoyment of it outweigh the costs, in terms of energy and money, of acquiring it?" There's a balance between purchasing material possessions we will enjoy versus simplifying our lives and minimizing their burden. For example, high-quality items that we love and that have good energy affect us positively. So it may be worth spending the extra money for a higher-quality item. When you are clear about your values and priorities, you will know where this balance lies.

One area we spend valuable energy on is our homes. Statistics reveal that since 1950, the average new house has increased by 1,247 square feet. Meanwhile, the average household has shrunk by one person. The bigger the house we own, the more time, energy, and money goes into maintaining, cleaning, heating, and decorating it. Not to mention buying furniture to fill the extra space. Further, although a larger house provides more privacy, it also diminishes intimacy, as family members are more spread out. You are paying for this extra space with your vital life-force energy. Is it worth it? How much room do you really need?

While living on a sailboat for six months, my husband and I quickly adjusted to living in a smaller space and found that we had more time and energy for life-enhancing activities like connecting with people and nature, exploring the countries we visited, and reading and writing. After returning, we lived in a one-bedroom bungalow near the beach for two years, and it felt large compared to the boat. It's all a matter of perspective.

Another area we spend a tremendous amount of our resources on is our vehicles. The cost of maintenance, gas, insurance, and registration is quite high when you think of how many hours you have to work to pay for it. You may want to sit down and do the math. What if you were to carpool, use public transportation, or ride a bike to work, eliminating one of your family's cars? By commuting with a spouse, you would be able to spend more quality time together. Just like having a smaller house promotes closeness, so does sharing a car. Besides that, it forces you to communicate about your needs and plan time according to your values and priorities. Furthermore, think of the effect on our environment if we all did this!

Several months before leaving Seattle, John and I sold one of our vehicles and carpooled to work. Sharing a car, we spent more quality time together and found it very satisfying. Upon returning from our voyage, we shared a car again. We purposefully found an apartment close to a bus stop so John could either ride his bike or take the bus to work. The money we saved on gas, maintenance, registration, and insurance made it worth any inconveniences we encountered.

We are programmed by the media to believe bigger, newer, faster, and better is the way to go, and therefore we spend valuable resources on things we don't really need or truly desire just to keep up with the Joneses. There is nothing wrong with having nice things to enjoy, but it's important to consider the cost in terms of your vital life-force energy.

Eliminate Credit-Card Debt

Debt is consuming our country and robbing us of our freedom, creativity, and passion. Our life-force energy gets bound into paying it off: the items purchased are no longer being used but still being paid for, and we are paying more than the amount originally owed, once the interest is added. This behavior doesn't make sense, and yet it is viewed as normal in our society. According to the Federal Reserve Survey of Consumer Finances for 2004, 46.2 percent of American families carry a balance on their credit cards. The average balance in 2004 was $5,100, a 15.9 percent increase from 2001. Making matters worse, the younger generations are enticed by the media to purchase things *now* to look good or be popular, instead of saving for them. And credit cards are more readily available than ever before.

Never feeling satisfied with what we have and always wanting more is a common experience in our consumer-oriented culture and is the main reason for our problem with credit-card debt. This only perpetuates our obsessive behavior of overworking to pay for overspending. As a result, we are stressed and unfulfilled with our lives.

Feeling disconnected from ourselves, we attempt to fill the void by overspending, thus creating a vicious cycle.

In my mid-twenties, I experienced what it was like to be in credit-card debt without any money saved. I felt immobilized, burdened, and ashamed, and as a result, I decided to get help by joining a twelve-step Debtors Anonymous group, which helped me understand my spending habits and reasons for overspending. Consequently, I cut up my credit cards and vowed never to get into this position again. Currently, the only debt we carry is our mortgage. Even our cars are paid for. As a result, life is simpler and we have more energy to pursue our dreams and passions.

Take time to consider your spending habits. Are you overspending to keep up with the Joneses or to fill an emotional or spiritual void? If so, consider getting help by joining a support group like Debtors Anonymous or consulting with a credit-counseling or debt-consolidation service. Spend time daily expressing gratitude for what you already have. And remember: true wealth can only be measured by the quality of our lives, not the quantity of stuff we have.

By eliminating credit-card debt and expressing gratitude for what's in your life, you will experience more freedom, peace, and joy.

Clear the Clutter

Energy needs to flow and move, or it becomes stagnant. Clutter is a good example: when things pile up, like unopened mail or e-mail, the flow of energy is blocked. It's important that we clear old or unused items from our closets, desks, bookshelves, computers, drawers, and cars. When determining what to part with, remember that material objects have an energy vibration, so surround yourself with things that you love and that reflect who you are—your unique style and tastes. Get rid of everything else. Recycle unread magazines; give away books that no longer interest you and clothes that no longer fit. Go through your entire house—every drawer and closet, every nook and cranny—at least once a year. If you haven't used or worn something in over a year, then it's likely you won't, so say goodbye.

When John and I moved to Big Bear, we downsized from a house to a 1,200-square-foot cabin and consequently got rid of a lot of stuff, like old pictures, wedding-gift crystal we never used, and hand-me-down furniture that didn't fit our style. As a result, when I had to evacuate our home due to the Old Fire in the fall of 2003, the process was much easier. (John was out of town at the time.)

Packing opened my eyes, as all of our treasured possessions, including a large dog and two cats, fit into a four-door Honda Accord. Everything else could easily be replaced. Also, from the time a mandatory evacuation was announced, I was out the door in just over an hour, and my drive off the mountain took about forty-five minutes. Later, I heard stories of people sitting in stand-still traffic for as long as five hours.

Driving away from our home toward safety, sadness overwhelmed me as I realized I might never see our house again. On the other hand, it was liberating to know that everything that was *really* important to me was safe and that I had all I needed to start over.

Cindy, a fifty-year-old holistic health therapist who enjoys helping others simplify their homes and lives, felt liberated when moving from Ohio to California with all of her earthly possessions in a van. "It feels good, it keeps things light," she exclaimed.

After getting divorced and leaving her home of many years, she shared, "I have no attachment to material things." She has only a few pieces of furniture and is happier than ever. "I love my life right now," Cindy said, smiling.

When meeting with clients to help simplify the clutter in their lives, Cindy asks, "What do you think about this item? Do you love it? Does it have sentimental value? How does it make you feel?" Cindy encourages them to keep only what they love, what has sentimental value, and what makes them feel good.

Take time to go through all of the items in your house and ask yourself the above questions. Pretend you are moving in one month, and get rid of everything you don't want to take with you—things that have old energy, that you don't love, or that aren't useful. If you have difficulty with this process, there may be underlying emotional issues making it difficult for you to let go. Consider seeking help from a therapist to process and resolve these issues so you can move forward with freedom and joy.

By simplifying the clutter in your life, you are increasing the flow of energy in your home and creating more room for your heart's desires to manifest.

Release the Past

The clutter in our lives only bogs down our energy and distracts us from what's really important. This is also true for our past—when we have emotional issues stemming from past hurts, we carry them like baggage into all areas of our lives, which affects our relationships, our work lives, and how we feel on a day-to-day basis, thus cluttering our existence. Our emotional baggage also causes more suffering as we continue to repeat the same patterns and mistakes. For example, if you were mistreated in a romantic relationship, you will likely project feelings of anger and distrust onto your next relationship—thus causing unnecessary suffering for you and your partner—if you don't work on understanding, forgiving, and letting go of the first relationship.

Psychotherapy is helpful in processing and understanding our painful experiences so we can heal resentments, forgive others and ourselves, and move on with our lives. It takes courage, and the process of letting go of the past can take time—like peeling an onion, you may shed one layer to find there is yet another underneath. So, it's important to be patient and loving with yourself. It's also important to release emotions in a constructive way, such as through tears, laughter, or healthy outbursts of anger. The following are suggestions for releasing pent-up tears:

- Watch a sad movie alone with a Kleenex box by your side. Allow yourself to bawl your eyes out, releasing from deep within.

- Since our emotions can get stored in our bodies, schedule an appointment with a body worker, such as a massage therapist, whom you trust.

- Listen to music that touches your heart.

- View something of great beauty that moves you, such as a landscape or painting.

- Look at a picture of a deceased loved one.

If you have unresolved feelings of hurt, anger, or resentment, take time to journal for clarity, understanding, and awareness. Next, write a letter to the person with whom you are angry. Tell them exactly how you feel, releasing your emotions onto the paper. Burn the letter. Then write another letter, this time from a less angry and emotional place, and consider mailing or giving it to the person. Also, while meditating, visualize the person you are angry with sitting across from you, and talk to them. Speak from your heart without holding back. What might their response be? Try to imagine you are the other person. What are they feeling? Attempt to put yourself in their shoes to develop compassion.

If you are carrying a tremendous amount of anger, it may help to release it first. Here are some suggestions:

- Walk fast, run, or exercise with intensity.
- Chop wood.
- Beat on drums.
- Build something by pounding nails.
- Yell and scream into a pillow.
- Throw rocks where it's safe and no one will get hurt.

Tears may surface as you release and let go of your pain. Allow them to flow, as they will transform your anger into compassion and forgiveness. Forgiveness sets us and the other person free, allowing room for more joy and love in our lives.

Maybe you are having trouble forgiving yourself for your behavior in the past. Allow your anger toward yourself to come out in a letter, sharing your thoughts and feelings about what you did. Next, write a letter to your inner child—the innocent and vulnerable part of you. What would you say to this child? What have you learned from your mistakes? Remember, you were doing the best that you could at the time with the knowledge and wisdom you had. If others were hurt by your actions, consider making amends by apologizing in person or in a letter. This will allow room for love, compassion, forgiveness, and understanding to emerge.

Grief due to the loss of a loved one is another example of emotional baggage from the past that can drain our vital energy. Since it can take years to heal from this type of loss, it is imperative that we honor our own process. This means we need to take the time to grieve when feelings arise, let go of all expectations about how long it "should" take, and completely honor and care for ourselves. For example, allow yourself to take a nap when feeling tired, instead of beating yourself up by saying, "What's wrong with me? I shouldn't be so tired." Journal or talk to a close friend when feeling down, instead of drinking a bottle of wine. And trust that your energy, vitality, and joy will return over time.

As you consciously work on letting go of the old by prioritizing your life-force energy, choosing supportive relationships, simplifying material possessions, eliminating credit-card debt, and clearing the physical and emotional clutter from your life, you will create more room for new, fulfilling life experiences. You will then be well prepared to depart for your journey.

Exercises

1. Notice how you feel when spending your life-force energy. Are you energized, or do you feel drained? What are your core values? What's important to you? Are you currently living in alignment with your highest values? If not, what needs to change? Explain.

2. Make a list of each of your primary relationships. Write *positive*, *neutral*, or *negative* next to each person's name based on how they affect you and whether or not they support you living authentically and following your dreams. Describe any "negative" relationships. What can you do to neutralize their effects? Or do you need to move on and let them go?

3. Pay off credit-card debt. Create a spending plan of how you *want* to spend your money according to your values and priorities. Track your expenses to gain clarity on where you are overspending, and

work on understanding the underlying reasons. Consider seeking help through Debtors Anonymous or consulting with a credit-counseling or debt-consolidation service.

4. Clear out the clutter from your house, office, and car. Set up an annual spring-cleaning time. If you're not using something, you don't love it, or it doesn't have sentimental value, then get rid of it. Put an expiration date on items you have trouble discarding and let them go when the date arrives.

5. Do you have unresolved emotional issues from your past that are weighing you down? If so, consider seeking professional help from a therapist or healer, reading self-help books, journaling for awareness, or writing a letter to the person with whom you are angry, including yourself. Take steps to gain a deeper awareness of how your past is influencing your life today. Work on healing, forgiveness, and letting go.

Guided Meditation

The purpose of this meditation is to assist you in gaining clarity about what is draining your energy and to visualize releasing it.

Sit comfortably in a chair or cross-legged on a cushion on the floor with your back upright and your hands resting on your lap. Begin by bringing your focus of awareness inside to the core of your being. Notice your breath and allow it to deepen with each inhalation. Create a rhythmic flow by equally spacing your in-breath and out-breath. As you begin to relax, notice any areas in your body that feel tense or uncomfortable, and send breath to them, allowing the tension to soften and release. Next, notice the quality of your thoughts. Attempt to still your mind as you sit peacefully in silent awareness.

Examine your relationships. Are there people in your life who are draining your energy? Are you maintaining friendships that are no longer supporting you? Imagine all of the things draining your life-force energy: financial worries, unfinished items on your to-do list, clutter, unresolved emotional issues from your past. Take several moments to visualize placing all of these things in separate boxes.

Place each box in a pile in your driveway or in another open area outside. Add crumpled-up newspaper and small sticks for kindling, pour lighter fluid on the pile, light a match, and create a huge bonfire. Stand aside and watch. As the flames burn through the items in each box, imagine more space and energy being created for all of your deepest dreams and desires. Notice how you feel: are you beginning to feel lighter? As you let go of the items in each box, imagine what you would like to bring into your life, like better health, fulfilling new relationships, or financial abundance. When the last box has burned, visualize in detail how you want your life to look and how you desire *to feel. Express gratitude as if the transformation has already taken place.*

When you feel complete, slowly and gently bring yourself back to the room and open your eyes. Record your experience and any new insights that occurred to you. List in order of priority the projects you would like to accomplish or what you need to let go of to create room for the life of your dreams.

PART III

DEPART
FOR
DISTANT SHORES

UP-ANCHOR AND RAISE THE SAILS

» *Participate in Life*

Greatness is not in where we stand, but in what direction we are moving. We must sail sometimes with the wind and sometimes against it—but sail we must and not drift, nor lie at anchor.

—OLIVER WENDELL HOLMES

September 6, 1998. It is the sixth day of an eleven-day passage from the country of Vanuatu to Cairns, Australia. I just got off my 2:30–4:00 a.m. watch. It was great! The autopilot worked, winds were low, and the swells small. Most importantly, we picked up a new passenger—a bird. I got to see it land gracefully on the bow after several attempts. Without everyday distractions such as answering phone calls, checking e-mail, and watching TV, life has really slowed down and I'm able to experience the richness in simple things. I feel content and at peace.

Take Control of the Helm

To participate in life means to take control of our sailboat's helm and consciously navigate a safe passage, making decisions that are in alignment with who we are and our life purpose. If we let go of the helm and let the wind, waves, and currents guide us, allowing life to happen to us, we will be lost at sea and never reach our desired destination.

One way we let go of the helm is by allowing distractions such as watching television, getting unexpected phone calls, checking e-mail, surfing the Internet, and talking on the cell phone to keep us from achieving our goals. For example, today I woke up around eight a.m., attended to my pets, made a fire, checked voice mail and e-mail, and then received a phone call that lasted forty-five minutes, and then another call that lasted half an hour. Then, while eating breakfast, I heard a suspicious squeaking noise downstairs, only to find my cat had brought home a mouse. After attending to the mouse—catching it, making sure it wasn't injured, accidentally losing it in the house, catching it again, and releasing it somewhere safe—another forty-five minutes had vanished. The day was half over, and I had only written one paragraph!

Sometimes we aren't able to control the distractions that show up in our lives, like the mouse in my house, but by consciously taking control of the helm, we can choose which ones to pay attention to. For instance, I didn't have to answer both phone calls. We can choose to set boundaries about how much TV we watch, when we have the cell phone turned on, or how much time we spend on the Internet. Freeing ourselves from the influence of addiction will also help us to be more present. And living a balanced lifestyle will give us the energy we need to participate fully in life.

Taking control of the helm is about waking up and becoming conscious of our decisions and behaviors so that we can navigate a safe passage to living a more purposeful life. Now that we know who we are, what we want, and where we're headed on our journey, and now that we've created room for the life we desire, we need to eliminate distractions and choose a healthy lifestyle so we can up-anchor, raise the sails, and sail into the life of our dreams.

Unplug from TV

Statistics by ACNielsen reveal that the average American watches over four hours of television per day, which equals about twenty-eight hours per week, or nine years in a sixty-five-year life. Watching TV on a regular basis is a predominant way we give up the helm in our lives. The physical, psychological, emotional, and spiritual costs are great, not to mention the opportunity costs with all of that time spent watching moving images instead of participating in life and going after our dreams.

Before John and I left Seattle in 1998, we spent an average of about fifteen to twenty hours per week in front of the TV. We recognized that this behavior was only adding to our feelings of discontentment by stifling our creativity and taking time away from developing friendships and community—all the things that could provide real fulfillment. Consequently, we made several attempts to cut down on the amount of television we watched, including putting the TV in the closet and taking it out only on "sick days." We also called to have the cable disconnected. (No one ever showed up, so we kept receiving cable, for free.) As none of these tactics really worked, we finally decided to give our TV away when departing for our travels.

While sailing overseas, we had very little contact with television, other than watching an occasional rugby or soccer game at a local pub. Then, one day, five months into our journey, friends of the captain's son put us up in a fancy resort hotel in Bali, Indonesia. Lo and behold, the suite had a television. Following an exhausting passage from Gili Island to Bali, in which we made very slow progress against twenty-knot headwinds and a two-knot current, we were excited to isolate ourselves in our hotel room and lie in bed. We were especially anxious for some time alone after spending the previous five months on the sailboat, living in close quarters with little privacy. TV was the perfect escape.

Two hours of channel flipping between boring programs led to feelings of irritability. My neck became tense and stiff, and I realized I had felt this way frequently when living in Seattle. This irritability and tension caused me to feel edgy and dissatisfied. I knew immediately its source and couldn't believe how obvious it was after only a couple of hours. It occurred to me the television may have created an overload on my mental circuits, since life had slowed down so much while living at sea. I wondered, "If only two hours of television could cause me to feel this awful, then what were the effects of watching every day? What about people who watched even more than I did?" Needless to say, our decision to part with our TV was reconfirmed.

Tommy, a nineteen-year-old college student, grew up without a television in his home. Since he had very little exposure to it, he didn't feel the need for it. Tommy shared, "Not having TV as a kid, I have a wide span of talents." He is a brilliant student and talented athlete, skateboarder, waterskier, surfer, and musician. Without the television taking up his time, he was able to focus his energy on school and develop skills for the things he loves, as well as spend a lot of time outdoors.

Tommy continued, "Without TV telling you what you should have, you don't feel the need to have all the toys. By not having all the latest toys, you find things that are more true to who you are." Tommy sees his friends conforming to the latest fads, purchasing the newest toys, and playing popular video games. Since he wasn't under the influence of television, he has developed unique and authentic interests and talents that he feels passionate about.

Adjusting to living in the dorms with a roommate who has the television on frequently has been a challenge for Tommy. When he walks in the room and the TV is on, he feels tension. Tommy said, "TV creates that tension where you can't even relax. The energy of it is very distracting and unnerving. It makes me feel irritable and stuck so that I lose my creativity and inspiration."

Tommy added, "TV fills time but doesn't fuel your mind or enjoyment in life."

It also keeps us from taking risks, causing us to be passive bystanders. For instance, instead of watching a baseball game on television, why not attend the game and experience the excitement and energy of the crowd? Better yet, why not join a recreational baseball team and *really* participate by getting exercise and experiencing camaraderie with your teammates? Instead of watching the Travel Channel, save the money you would have spent on cable to travel. (For example, let's say cable costs you $40 a month: you could save $480 a year toward travel expenses.) Notice how this makes you feel more adventurous and alive!

If it's too scary to part with your beloved television, try going on a "TV diet." Start by keeping a written record of how much time you spend watching over a one-week period. Then, create a plan that honors your values and priorities—how you *want* to spend your life-force energy. Maybe it includes viewing TV one hour a night instead of two, or only on weekends, so you can spend more time exercising, reading, hanging out with friends, or doing artwork. Consider videotaping your favorite shows and fast-forwarding through the commercials to cut down on the amount of time spent watching, as well as the *stuff* your mind has to process. This also allows you to control when to turn it on, so you don't rush through dinner just to catch a show. Or do as I did and get a TV/VCR combo or DVD player to view movies only.

While creating your plan, include a list of activities you would like to do in place of watching TV, like taking a class, gardening, or meditating. Make sure to include time to just relax and be still. Further, ask a friend to hold you accountable so you don't unconsciously slip back into your old behavior patterns and let go of the helm. For instance, in the past maybe you set your intentions to watch a half-hour sitcom, but as you sank deeper into the couch on a rainy day, you found a good movie, and then another. The next thing you knew, your entire day was spent in front of the TV. With a plan in place and a friend to hold you accountable, you are more likely to make conscious choices to participate in life.

Also, keep in mind the quality of shows you watch. For instance, notice how you feel after watching the news versus a funny comedy. Do violent movies cause you to feel irritable and sleep poorly? Remember, what you put in your mind affects how you feel: just as eating junk food causes you to feel bad, so does viewing violent or disturbing TV shows and movies.

Write the following quote by Bob Moawad, an author, motivational speaker, and business consultant, on an index card and tape it where you can see it (on or near the TV, perhaps): "You can't leave footprints in the sands of time if you're sitting on your butt—and who wants to leave buttprints in the sands of time?"

To truly experience the richness of life, unplug the TV, follow your heart, and fully participate in activities you feel passionate about. As you do, your self-esteem and outlook on life will improve, and you will be well on your way to living a more purposeful life.

Set Boundaries with Your Cell Phone

According to the Cellular Telecommunications and Internet Association (CTIA), from 1995 to 2005 the overall number of wireless phone subscribers in the United States increased by more than 600 percent. More than 190 million people now use wireless services, compared to fewer than 30 million ten years ago. With this substantial increase in usage, our lives have changed. Not only do we have more conveniences at our fingertips, we are more distracted than ever before. Our energy is spread out, rather than being fully present and engaged with what we are doing and whom we are with, including ourselves. For example, when our cell phones are turned on all the time, we are constantly distracted from being in the moment, even if on a subconscious level, because we are waiting for the next call. If we are talking to someone in person, the minute the phone rings, our connection with that person is lost and our attention is taken away, somewhere else. Equally important, if we are talking on the phone when driving home from work, our alone time is diminished—we could be using this time to process our day.

Not only does our cell phone keep us from being fully present with others and ourselves, but our privacy is frequently invaded. For example, while I was waiting at the airport for a flight during the holidays, the lady next to me was talking on her cell phone. Attempting to read, I was able to hear every word of her conversation and became frustrated. I was temporarily relieved because she finally got up to leave, but then yet another lady sat down in her place and made a call. She talked about her family, health problems, the new kitchen floor, grandkids, and Christmas plans—all her personal business. Feelings of irritation came over me as my own personal space continued to be invaded.

Besides being an intrusion on our privacy, downtime, and intimate connections with others, cell phones have been found to cause an increase in traffic accidents when used while driving. A study in Perth, Australia, found that motorists who used cell phones while driving were four times as likely to get into crashes serious enough to injure themselves. Recently, there has been an increase in driver-distraction legislation, and most experts agree that the rapid growth of new wireless technologies in the driving environment—most notably cell phones—is responsible. The following are suggestions for minimizing your risk of accidents involving a cell phone:

- Turn off your phone or always keep it freely accessible in the car so you don't have to fumble for it when it rings.

- Pull off the road, if possible, before answering or placing a call.

- Use an earpiece when talking while driving to keep your hands free.

- Focus on driving even if it means you miss a call or disconnect abruptly.

- Avoid high-stress, emotional conversations while driving—not only with cell-phone callers, but with passengers as well.

When considering how to set boundaries with your cell phone, think about your values and priorities. If you value your intimate connections with others, then turn off your cell phone when having a face-to-face conversation. If you value your alone time, then turn off your phone while driving to and from work, when exercising, or while eating a meal. Better yet, turn on your cell phone only when you are expecting a call or when you need to place a call. Otherwise, keep it turned off so you can be fully present and engaged in life. This goes for your home phone as well. Instead of answering the phone every time it rings, why not let your voice mail pick it up, unless you are expecting the call. Or turn off the ringer while sleeping, eating, or conversing with loved ones. Take control of the helm and don't allow the phone to dictate how you spend your valuable time and life-force energy.

Limit Your Time on the Internet

Another way we give up the helm is by indiscriminately using the Internet. How often have you logged on to the Internet to look something up or check e-mail only to find yourself half an hour later absorbed in a website you had no intention of looking at? Do you compulsively check e-mail ten times a day even though your in-box is empty? Some people I know have hundreds of e-mails sitting in their in-box waiting to be read and sorted through. This takes a tremendous amount of time and mental energy that could be spent working toward your dreams. What about those e-mails that just sit there waiting to be read later but that you never get to? Every time you see them, they remind you that you have unfinished business—another thing on your to-do list—and your life-force energy gets slowly drained. If they aren't important, delete them. Be discerning about what you look at. Think of what you could do with all the time you spend reading forwarded e-mails or advertisements!

The Internet is an amazing tool that provides convenience to our lives and that *can* save us time and energy.

For instance, shopping or doing research online saves valuable time in not having to drive to the store or library. For most people, the Internet is simply a tool used for communication and gathering information. But for others, it can become a substitute for real-life relationships and a threat to financial and emotional well-being.

Brandon, a twenty-four-year-old college student, spends between five to eight hours a day playing an interactive computer game on the Internet. He has no job or girlfriend, his grades are sliding, and he doesn't want to go out anymore. Brandon shared, "It occupies my life and my thoughts. I think about it for an hour before falling asleep at night and stay up late playing." Although Brandon feels his life is out of balance, he admits to being addicted and doesn't want to stop playing.

When we *unconsciously* engage in watching television, surfing the Internet, or playing computer games, valuable time is eaten up. These physically passive activities take us away from socially interacting with people and pursuing our dreams. It's important to *consciously* take control of the helm and set boundaries that are true to who you are and your deepest values and priorities instead of allowing the winds of distraction to blow you off course from your desired destination.

Free Yourself from Addiction

Addiction uses up an incredible amount of time and life-force energy, causing us to be distracted by always thinking ahead: *When and where am I going to get my next fix?* It also blocks our creative process and spiritual growth, keeping us stuck and feeling unfulfilled. As a result, we give up the helm and are unable to be present and participate fully in life.

According to *Merriam-Webster's Dictionary*, the definition of *addiction* is "a compulsive need for and use of a habit-forming substance characterized by tolerance and by well-defined physiological symptoms upon withdrawal." The most notable addiction is chemical dependency—substances such as drugs, alcohol, and nicotine. But there are also many other forms of addiction that keep us from living fully, such as addictions to gambling, sex, food, shopping, and overworking. We are addicted to anything we engage in compulsively that controls our thoughts and behaviors, despite the destructive consequences it has on our relationships, finances, health, and well-being.

One area of addiction that isn't well acknowledged is in new technologies, such as the Internet, television, and video and computer games. These have been found to tap our already obsessive-compulsive natures. For example, according to Robert Kubey, Rutgers University psychologist and TV-Free America board member, once the television is turned on, it's difficult to turn off. Many viewers exhibit the same symptoms as shown by substance abuse, such as (1) using TV as a sedative, (2) indiscriminate viewing, (3) feeling loss of control while viewing, (4) feeling angry with self for watching too much, (5) inability to stop watching, and (6) feeling miserable when kept from watching. According to Marie Winn in *The Plug-In Drug*, "Television's attraction is so powerful precisely because it gratifies the passive side of human nature that everyone is endowed with in differing degrees." So television taps not only our compulsive nature, but our tendency toward being passive as well.

Even though using the Internet and playing video and computer games are less passive activities than watching TV, they still keep us from *really living*. Now there is even scientific evidence to suggest that video-game playing is physically addictive. In a study conducted at the Hammersmith Hospital in London, researchers found that playing video games doubles the amount of dopamine production in the brain. This increase is roughly the same as when a person is injected with amphetamines or Ritalin—in other words, equivalent to a dose of speed.

Oftentimes, we use addictions to distract us and emotionally numb out so we don't have to face feelings of discontentment, such as anger, fear, grief, boredom, and loneliness. Unfortunately, this behavior only adds to our feelings of dissatisfaction, thus creating a cycle that can be extremely difficult to break the pattern of.

What causes you to disappear, numb out, or not participate? Maybe it's watching TV, surfing the Internet, or using substances. Do these things take your attention away from what's really important or keep you stuck from moving forward in life? Ask yourself, "Am I living life to the fullest? Do I feel satisfied, vibrant, and alive?" If not, then track how much time you spend on activities that keep you from really living. How many hours a day or week do you do these things? What are the opportunity costs in terms of creative endeavors, recreational activities, physical vitality, and intimate relationships? How is it affecting your body, mind, and spirit? Are you using it to avoid feelings of discontentment? In what ways can you participate more fully in your life?

Maybe you aren't addicted to new technology or substances but are living a fast-paced life with little downtime and are overstimulating your mind. While driving, you talk on the cell phone or think about your to-do list. When you slow down on the weekend, you crave stimulation and watch TV or surf the Internet just to keep busy. This cycle of busyness is like being on a treadmill: it's difficult to get off, so you keep going and going. Even when you have a still moment while waiting for a plane or sitting in traffic, you have to be doing something, checking something, or calling someone, which causes your energy to be scattered and unfocused. In the process, you are taken out of the moment and miss the richness of life. Furthermore, staying busy is another way of avoiding discontentment. If the above description fits you, what are you avoiding? What are you afraid of?

As you begin to slow down and eliminate the distractions in your life, more space will be created for your desires to manifest. Initially, you may feel a void, which can be uncomfortable, but it is from this void that infinite possibilities are born. So be patient with the process and allow for the emptiness—the space. It is from this place of stillness and silence that your soul is able to speak to you about what will fulfill you and add purpose to your life.

Choose a Healthy, Balanced Lifestyle

Saying no to distractions and prioritizing how you *want* to spend your time and energy will help you participate more fully in life, but if your life is still unbalanced and your health is questionable, you won't have the energy to be fully present and engaged. Therefore, it's important to choose a healthy, balanced lifestyle for all areas of your life—body, mind, and soul.

Feeding your body with fresh, natural foods like organic fruits and vegetables will give you more energy while clearing your mind and making it easier to connect to your spirit. Too often, we eat excessive sugar or drink caffeine to keep up with the frantic pace we've set. This may give us temporary energy, but ultimately our blood sugar will crash, causing us to feel tired and crave more. As we continue to use stimulants like sugar and caffeine to keep us going, our bodies eventually give up and get sick. Frequently eating out or eating fast food is another way we deprive ourselves of good nutrition and health. By creating room in your lifestyle to prepare healthy meals, you are giving yourself a huge gift that will last a lifetime.

Exercising regularly will increase your immune system response, improve your mood, make you stronger, and add to your vitality. Pick an exercise program that works best for you. Maybe it's walking every day in the morning or mixing it up by jogging, hiking, swimming, biking, going to the gym, doing yoga, or taking a dance class. Whatever program or routine you choose, make it enjoyable. Schedule walking or hiking dates with friends to motivate you while also fulfilling your social needs, giving you a "two for one," as my mom would say.

Feed your mind with positive, life-enhancing information. As mentioned earlier, when we watch violence on the news or television shows, our mood is affected, often becoming irritable or depressed. Watch funny movies or educational shows instead, or choose news programs that don't sensationalize the negative. Read inspiring and uplifting books and stories. Set boundaries with what you take into your mind, and don't waste time looking at junk mail, junk e-mail, or TV commercials. These things fill your mind with unnecessary information, taking space that could be used for realizing your dreams.

Feed your spirit by surrounding yourself with people, places, and things that you love. Create a sanctuary in your home, a place where you feel relaxed, rejuvenated, and peaceful. Hang pictures or poems that inspire you, and play uplifting, soulful music. Chapter 6 will go into more detail about how to connect with your spirit and nurture your soul.

Where in your life are you out of balance? What are you feeding your body, mind, and soul? Maybe you spend too much time working and not enough time being with your family or exercising and taking care of your health. Without your health, nothing else matters!

How do you nurture your soul? What is the quality of the information you allow into your mind? Take time to evaluate the important areas in your life and create an action plan for creating a healthy balance. For example, leave work a half hour earlier to make time to exercise; cut back to one cup of coffee a day or switch to decaf; chart your meals for an entire week and figure out ways to decrease processed foods and add more fresh fruits and vegetables; instead of watching the news before going to bed, read an inspirational book.

Slow down. Turn off your TV, computer, and cell phone. Watch the sunset, go for a walk with your loved ones, spend time in nature, take a dance class, or volunteer. Have intimate conversations with your partner. Read a good book, play games, paint a picture, write a book—pursue your dreams. Ask yourself, "If I were on my deathbed, would I regret missing an episode of *Desperate Housewives*, or would it be the time I didn't spend fulfilling my deepest desires?" What are your unfulfilled dreams? Take steps now to participate fully in your life so you can realize your dreams.

By waking up and making conscious decisions about how you spend your time and energy, you are in control of the helm and are able to up-anchor, raise the sails, and navigate a safe passage to living a more purposeful life.

Exercises

1. Calculate the number of hours a week you spend watching TV. Create a "TV diet" by giving yourself permission to watch a certain amount per day or per week, or only specific shows of interest. Then, stick to your new diet. As you reduce the amount of time spent in front of the TV, notice how you feel. Do you feel more alive? With the time you used to spend watching TV, sign up for a recreational sports team,

take a class, have a friend over for dinner, play games with your partner, read books, or go on a walk. Be creative and try something new that you've always wanted to do.

2. Set specific boundaries with your cell phone depending on your needs, values, and priorities. For example, practice turning it off while driving or having a face-to-face conversation with someone. Notice whether you are able to be more relaxed and present.

3. Track how much time you spend on the Internet checking e-mail, surfing websites, playing games, and so on. Do this every day for a week. Pay attention to how much of your time is leaking away. Create limits on how often you check e-mail and use the Internet.

4. If you are struggling with addiction, consider seeking help. Join a support group, work with a reputable therapist or hypnotherapist, and educate yourself as much as possible about your particular addiction and the most effective methods of treatment. Depending on its severity, you may want to research treatment facilities covered by your insurance.

5. On an 8½ × 11 inch piece of paper, make three columns, titled "Body," "Mind," and "Soul." Under each column, write all of the positive things you are

doing to nurture each in your life. Every day, make it a challenge to add to your list. Ask yourself what you can do to create a more healthy and balanced lifestyle. Meditate and journal for clarity.

Guided Meditation

This meditation is designed to help you experience being still, without distractions, and to clarify ways in which you can participate more fully in your life.

Sit comfortably in a chair or cross-legged on a cushion on the floor with your back upright and your hands resting on your lap. Begin by bringing your focus of awareness inside to the core of your being. Notice your breath and allow it to deepen with each inhalation. Create a rhythmic flow by equally spacing your in-breath and out-breath. As you begin to relax, notice any areas in your body that feel tense or uncomfortable, and send breath to them, allowing the tension to soften and release. Next, notice the quality of your thoughts. Attempt to still your mind as you sit peacefully in silent awareness.

Imagine you are alone on a sailboat. It's a beautiful, sunny day with light winds and small swells. You've plotted a course to your desired destination and autopilot is in control of the helm, so you are lying in the cockpit and basking in the warmth of the sun. Take a deep breath and sigh as you exhale. The sun beams down, relaxing your body as you sink deeper into the cockpit cushions. Experience the gentle rocking of the boat as it rides the waves, the wind filling your sails, propelling you forward. Hear the gurgling sound of the water splashing on the hull. Watch the sky for birds and clouds. Without distractions such as your television, cell phone, or computer, you are free to just be. Relax and feel the bliss of being still, in the moment.

Picture yourself in perfect health—strong, whole, and full of vitality. If you experience any tension, discomfort, or dis-ease in your body, notice it melting away with each breath. Feel the lightness of your being. See yourself eating healthy foods and exercising regularly. You are in a wonderful mood and feel really good about yourself because you have chosen a completely balanced and stress-free lifestyle.

Visualize yourself fully participating in life. What does it look like? Are you engaging with people you love, involved with your community, traveling, or participating in fun activities? What are the things you've always dreamed of doing? See yourself doing them now. Take a moment to pause and picture the details. Notice how you feel. Are you more present? Do you feel alive, awake, and focused? Take in this awesome vision . . . and know you are sailing into the life of your dreams.

When you feel complete, slowly and gently bring yourself back to the room and open your eyes. Record your experience and any new insights that occurred to you. How can you participate more fully in your life?

SAIL AWAY FROM THE SAFE HARBOR

» *Take Risks*

Twenty years from now you will be more
disappointed by the things that you didn't
do than by the ones you did do. So throw off
the bowlines. Sail away from the safe harbor.
Catch the trade winds in your sails. Explore.
Dream. Discover.

—MARK TWAIN

*A*ugust 21, 1998. *Sailing from Fiji to Vanuatu, I am alone on my 2:30 a.m. watch. It is pitch black outside, except for the whitecaps breaking near the stern of the boat. My heart is pounding and every muscle in my body is tense as I clutch the companionway and jam my foot up against the steering console to brace myself in as the waves violently lift and drop the boat. This is my first ocean passage, first time away from the sight of land, and my first storm at sea. Despite being afraid, I feel exhilarated and excited by the force of the wind and waves.*

Leave Your Comfort Zone

Sailing away from the safe harbor is about leaving the comfort zone of our lives, venturing into the unknown—uncharted waters—and taking risks. When John and I left Seattle to follow our dreams and travel overseas, we encountered several storms. With each storm came feelings of anxiety, but also, never had we felt so alive. Witnessing the power of nature and the ocean was an awesome experience, and we had an incredible sense of accomplishment when arriving unharmed at the other side. Even though we took appropriate precautions like checking the weather report before leaving for our destination, harnessing in when seas were rough, and traveling during the safest time of year, we still encountered stormy weather.

When leaving our comfort zone, we are able to get out of the box and re-create our lives according to what feels right and good to us. New experiences enliven and awaken us, heighten our senses, and stir our passions. That is why travel is on most people's list of things to do before they die. The reason I loved cruising so much is that I got to see things that normal tourists didn't—the island with no footprints on it, Komodo dragons in their natural habitat, villages of people living in harmony with the earth. I was able to get off the beaten path and experience totally new and exciting things, and spending time with people from different cultures and backgrounds stirred my creativity. My spirit came alive.

Purposely placing ourselves in new circumstances will feel uncomfortable at first, but the outcome is personal growth and a richer life. For example, while traveling, John and I didn't always know the etiquette of the cultures we visited or where we were going. But by witnessing how others lived, we learned valuable, life-altering lessons, making the discomfort well worth it. And if we got lost, we asked for directions. Sometimes getting lost was half the fun!

Whether it's exploring a new neighborhood, traveling to the other side of the world, or telling someone how you feel, sail away from the safe harbor and take risks. For the sailboat was built to leave the harbor, as you were made to create, explore, and live life to the fullest. If you remain secure, safe, and comfortable, you'll never know what could have happened—and you may regret not try-ing to find out.

Free Yourself from Limiting Beliefs

Limiting beliefs keep us from taking risks and prevent us from reaching for the stars, fulfilling our potential, and living fully and passionately. They keep us from moving forward and realizing our dreams.

What are limiting beliefs? They are beliefs that have been programmed in us to create negative or constricting thought and behavior patterns, often from the time we were young. They have been passed down through the generations of our families, such as, "Children should be seen and not heard." The consequence of such a belief early on might eventually produce another limiting be-lief: "If I speak my truth, I'll be punished." The resulting behavior pattern is *passivity*, the inability to speak up for oneself or be assertive.

Limiting beliefs are also passed on to us by our cul-ture—where we are in time and space according to what's going on, like our economic circumstances or global situ-ation. For example, the belief "There is not enough work (or money, and so on), so hoard what you have" may have served a purpose during the Great Depression in the 1930s, but it limits us today. Also, limiting beliefs are created from our personal life experiences. For instance, if you have a history of being hurt in romantic relation-ships, you may believe, "All romantic relationships are painful."

Since our beliefs create our thoughts, and our thoughts influence our behaviors and attract our experiences, we need to change our beliefs in order to create positive ex-periences. For example, if you have a limiting belief that says, "I'm not good enough," then it will be difficult for you to attract abundance in all areas of your life. You will also behave in ways to reinforce your negative be-lief. However, a belief like "I am completely worthy to receive good in my life" will attract wonderful, joyous ex-periences. Our unconscious mind always follows the in-structions of our beliefs and attempts to make them true, so it is imperative we be diligent about our beliefs.

As we grow and evolve, we need to upgrade our be-lief systems to support us rather than restrict us. We need to rewire our brains with new, constructive beliefs and thought patterns. The process begins with awareness. It may be helpful to explore your beliefs for each area in your life, such as relationships, money, and career. Get out several pieces of paper, and at the top of each one write, "My limiting beliefs about relationships are . . ." or "My limiting beliefs about money are . . ." Then, cre-ate a list for each area, forming a column on the left-hand side. Look at places where you feel stuck. Maybe you aren't attracting the type of relationship you desire.

Explore what your beliefs are about relationships. Do you feel you deserve to be happy in a relationship? Are you limiting yourself to how much love or joy you experience because you believe you are unworthy? As you become aware of the beliefs that no longer serve you, write down the new beliefs you would like to replace them with in the right-hand column, such as, "I am worthy of receiving abundant love." Also, write these new beliefs on an index card and make them visible to allow your subconscious mind to work on transforming them.

Limiting beliefs create fear and constriction. They take us away from experiencing love, joy, and abundance. When we break free from their chains, we tap into the universal source of infinite possibilities—the place where miracles are born.

Transform Fear

Like limiting beliefs, our fears, when left unconscious, keep us paralyzed and prevent us from taking risks. As we begin to live an authentic and purposeful life, it's common for our deepest fears to kick in. For example, when I began writing to be published, I faced the fear of being judged. What if people didn't like what I wrote or judged me personally? Once I faced my fear and allowed myself to be known through my writing, I realized I wasn't going to die from rejection, and my fear subsided.

Besides the common fear of failure is the fear of success—and having all of the responsibilities that come with it, such as more people looking up to and counting on us, less time to take care of ourselves, and less time to spend with loved ones. We may also fear having to leave our loved ones behind in the wake of our success, thus causing us to be "alone at the top."

Similar to our fear of success is the fear of being powerful. In *A Return to Love*, Marianne Williamson wrote, "Our deepest fear is not that we are inadequate. Our deepest fear is that we are powerful beyond measure. It is our light, not our darkness, that most frightens us." One of the greatest reasons we fear our light is because we fear death. Jesus's life is a good example. Being fully in his power and light, he was consequently crucified for fulfilling his purpose and speaking his truth. If we are in our power and living authentically, then we're in the spotlight. Not only might we be judged, but in the old days, we may have been killed. Obviously, this is an unconscious fear that no longer serves us today, but it still has power over us if it is not acknowledged.

When we come to understand that we won't die or be annihilated for being brilliant, then we are free to *really* live. Further, we need to know that death isn't the end, but rather a part of the cycle of creation and life. As we accept this fact, we are able to step out of our own box of self-imposed limitations and go after our dreams.

My mom, at the age of forty-one years old, was alone with her dad when he died from pneumonia due to being hospitalized with a cancerous brain tumor. She shared, "It was such a peaceful experience. Ever since then, I have not feared death." Consequently, my mom is someone who is not afraid to really live and experience all that life has to offer.

As you begin to live more authentically, sailing into uncharted waters, your fears will naturally surface like reefs, creating obstacles. When they do surface to threaten your journey, have great compassion for yourself and remember to breathe. Continue to move forward, knowing you are fully supported, and ask yourself, "What is the worst thing that could happen?" The more we face our fears and navigate through them, the stronger we become, and the more capable of facing the next challenge or fear that presents itself.

When not immobilizing, fear can be healthy, because it motivates us to move forward and take risks. It can also be telling us, "Stop! Don't do this thing." We need to listen carefully to its guidance: is there as an obstacle to be worked through, or are we heading for dangerous waters?

When preparing to leave Seattle, I had nightmares about tidal waves and experienced symptoms of anxiety, such as difficulty sleeping, tight shoulders, an upset stomach, and trouble concentrating. As I listened to my body, I realized my fear was about impending change. Like carefully navigating through a coral reef, I needed to honor my body and take it slowly during the process.

Gregg Levoy, in his book, *Callings*, talks about our resistance to change. He explains that we are naturally loath to part ways with the status quo, as we've spent years investing in job skills we've learned or relationships we've put energy into. As a result, we resist letting go, especially since there is no guarantee that change will be for the better.

Although resistance is uncomfortable and can keep us from moving forward, Levoy writes, "Resistance is also a good omen. It means you're close to something important, something vital for your soul's work here, something worthy of you."

Some signs of resistance are waiting for the right moment, self-sabotaging, distracting yourself with other activities, and making excuses such as, "I don't have enough time or money." If you experience resistance when going after your dreams, ask what its purpose is. Are you afraid of being seen and therefore judged? Are you afraid of your light and experiencing success? What will you have to give up, face, or change?

A powerful tool to release and transform the energy of fear is through fire ceremony. Begin by writing down your fears on a piece of paper. It may help to journal first for clarity. Then, start the ceremony by setting your intentions through prayer and meditation or developing a meaningful ritual. Be clear about what you wish to replace your fear with, such as love, joy, or confidence. Place your paper in a fire, or blow the energy of your fears into a small stick and throw that in the fire. This is all about setting your intentions, so be creative. A ceremony of this nature is more powerful when done during a new or full moon and with a group of people.

Fear, the opposite of love, is a belief in separation from God/Source/Life. Since God is love and we are made from love and one with God, fear is really an illusion, something we have learned along the way while playing the game of duality. Therefore, it's something we can unlearn.

Express Yourself in Relationships

One of the most difficult places to take risks is in our relationships. If we do so, though, we have the opportunity to experience deep meaning and purpose. But often, because we fear abandonment, rejection, or loss, we are too afraid to love deeply. We fear being alone in the world, so we hold back from expressing ourselves honestly and openly. This only perpetuates our fear and keeps us isolated and alone. Since we were meant to be in relationships with others—to connect with, work with, and have companionship and friendship with others—we must risk being known, even if we are ultimately rejected or abandoned or the other person passes away. Taking the risk to experience love is well worth it.

If you experience feelings of anger, hurt, or resentment in any of your relationships, take a risk and talk to the person, if it is safe to do so. But before you do, make a point to understand your part in what has happened. A relationship is dynamic, and the other person is often a mirror reflecting your own issues and insecurities. So be careful not to blame the other person and to *always* take responsibility for your part. Using "I" statements, such as, "I feel anxious when you come home late without calling," will help you take responsibility and keep the conversation constructive. If you attack the other person by yelling at them or saying, "You are always late," they will likely become defensive and yell back, thus creating a conflict. As a result, more anger will be invoked and nothing will get resolved. By taking responsibility when expressing yourself, the relationship has the opportunity to grow and become closer.

If you have unexpressed feelings for someone, risk telling them. For example, let's say you had a crush on someone in high school but never said anything—only to find out at your twenty-year reunion that they'd had a crush on you too. What would have happened? How would your life be different? You are not in high school anymore. Speak up! What do you have to lose?

When my father was hospitalized with cancer, my family and I visited him daily. We frequently told him we loved him when leaving the room. Being a quiet, reserved person, he had difficulty expressing his own sentiments. One time, however, he responded that he loved us too and then stated, "We should have said this more often." I wonder how much went unexpressed throughout the years.

Examine your relationships. Are you being open, honest, and vulnerable with the people who are important to you? Where are you holding back? Do you have unexpressed romantic feelings for someone? Is there someone with whom you feel angry? Stop playing it safe, and put yourself out there. Don't wait until the next natural disaster or until your loved ones are on their deathbeds to share from your heart. The reward is living a more purposeful life.

Know You Are Worthy

It takes not only courage but also positive self-esteem to take risks. People who are insecure feel unsafe stepping out of their comfort zone. Instead of facing their fears, they decide, "This is what I like," or "This is what I want," and they talk themselves into being happy. In the process, they become close-minded about the way life *should* be lived, as this adds to their feelings of safety and security. As a result, they live in a box of self-imposed limitations.

Knowing we are worthy is imperative to creating a purposeful life of our deepest dreams. If we give the Universe the message that we are unworthy of receiving our greatest good, then we will not attract it. In *Ask and It Is Given*, Esther and Jerry Hicks talk about the Law of Attraction, which says, "That which is like unto itself is drawn." The energy behind our thoughts, beliefs, and feelings about ourselves will attract life experiences with like energy. So, if we are judging and negative, we will attract people who are judging and experiences that are negative. If we are loving and positive, we will attract loving people and positive experiences.

Feeling worthy is about being able to ask for what we want, attract it to us, and then receive it. We all know the importance of giving, but without receiving, we have nothing to give. Therefore, it's important to consciously engage in the act of receiving. In *The Tao of Abundance*, Laurence Boldt suggests that receiving is an intentional act. Boldt says, "In order to receive, we must be willing to receive, which is another way of saying we must intend to receive. Intention implies both belief and action." An active way to demonstrate your intent and willingness to receive is to lay your hands on your lap with the palms facing open and upward while praying or meditating.

We all deserve to feel good and be happy. Since we are made from the same Source of all that is good, we can all readily tap into it. It is equally available to everyone at any time, not just a privileged few. When we feel worthy, we allow ourselves to receive from this Source of love, abundance, and well-being.

Do you feel worthy of receiving abundance—of manifesting your deepest dreams and desires? If not, you may need to learn how to love and honor yourself more. The following are exercises to assist you:

- Do five nice things for yourself every day, such as eat a healthy meal, go for a walk, take a bath, wear something you love, or go to bed early. Write them down in a "self-honoring journal" to keep track.

- Set aside "me time" daily to do something you enjoy, like reading, writing, painting, or exercising, even if only for ten or twenty minutes.

- Check in with yourself through prayer, meditation, and journaling to gain clarity about your needs.

- Take yourself on a "special date" once a week and go to the movies, an art gallery, or your favorite restaurant.

- Set boundaries with your time and energy according to your priorities, and say no to activities you are not excited about.

- Say or write the following affirmation: "I am lovable, acceptable, whole, and complete just as I am."

- Be assertive, ask for help, and accept it. You deserve all the support you need.

When loving and honoring yourself, be forgiving and compassionate when you make a mistake. Instead of judging or beating up on yourself when you do something you are unhappy with, like eating an entire box of cookies, acknowledge your feelings, let go of the past, and choose again. In every moment, we have the opportunity to make different, healthier choices. So, say to yourself, "I can choose again in this new moment."

Begin by noticing how you talk to yourself. What is your internal dialogue like? Are you loving and compassionate, or judging and hard? Do you frequently feel guilty? Guilt and self-criticism weigh us down, making us feel bad, and when we feel bad about ourselves, we often continue to make choices we are unhappy with. If you work on changing your thoughts, your actions will become more loving and compassionate. Likewise, if you change your actions to be more loving to yourself, like you will in doing the exercises above, then your thoughts will eventually change as well. You will be convincing your mind that you are worthy.

As you learn to love and honor yourself, your self-esteem and confidence will improve, you will have more courage to go after your dreams, and you will feel worthy of receiving all of the good available to you.

Choose to Take Risks

Every day, we have choices. We have choices about whether to play it safe or take risks, whether or not to get up and go to work in the morning, what to say or not to say to people we encounter throughout our day. We also have choices about what we think and what our attitude is toward life. People often hesitate to make choices because they fear making the wrong choice. But by consciously choosing, we can choose again.

Julie was a business analyst with the same company for thirteen and a half years. She knew the entire time that it wasn't a good fit. She shared, "My heart wasn't into it. I felt a little dead inside." Julie remained at the job because, as she said, "It was easy and I didn't know what else to do." She feared making the wrong choice.

Her biggest fear was about letting go of the financial security. She asked herself, "If I let go, where is the money going to come from?" Julie also had thoughts like, "Who do you think you are to take time off and not get paid?" Her family had instilled limiting beliefs in her about the importance of having a secure job. They didn't teach her that she could create her own life by doing what she loves.

Julie finally mustered the courage to quit her job after a few helpful nudges from friends and her own inner guidance. While at a party one night, she was complaining about her work, and a longtime friend said, "You've been saying that for twelve years now." This was an eye-opening experience, so she stopped complaining and decided to take action.

She also attended a workshop at which she received guidance during a meditation. "I had a vision I was falling and hands were catching me. I wasn't afraid and felt this sensation of trust. I had this overwhelming feeling that I needed to let go of my job in order to find what to do next." Processing her vision with friends only confirmed what her inner guidance was communicating to her.

Finally, on her thirty-ninth birthday, she realized she had been dissatisfied with her job for one-third of her life. Julie asked herself the question, "What if I were to die?" The process took time, like a sailboat tacking upwind, but eventually she decided to take a risk despite her fears.

Julie expected that leaving her job would be the greatest hurdle, but she is now being challenged with even more fears as she faces the unknown. She shared, "It's like I need to go through this initiation process." But by following her heart and working through her fears, her confidence and self-esteem continue to grow, and she's able to move forward in a positive direction.

Some helpful tools she is using during this time of uncertainty are journaling for clarity and insight, being open to what life presents, talking to friends, taking classes, and attending workshops. Julie said, "The process is different for each person, but the answers are always within."

Susie, the owner of the organic health-food store mentioned in Step 1, discussed what it was like to jump ship as a teacher to open her store: "Every step in the process was scary, because I didn't know what I was doing. It was all new territory." But despite her fears and the fears of others—as many people discouraged her from leaving the security of her teaching job—she forged ahead, knowing she was on the right path and fulfilling her purpose.

A year and a half later, Susie has taken another large risk by expanding her store despite not having the revenue flow from her business. She shared, "All along I've had a vision of my business being in this building, so when the opportunity came up to move, I knew it was meant to be, even though I didn't know how it was going to work out."

Susie explained that she is getting into an even larger financial obligation since she signed a lease option to buy the building in five years but doesn't yet know whether her business will grow enough to support it. Laughing, she stated, "I've got more money on the line now."

When asked how she handled her fears about expanding the store, she said with a relaxed tone, "I let go a lot more this time and was open to the idea that the vision will fulfill itself. Plus, I looked at it more objectively and wasn't emotionally committed to what I thought the outcome was going to be. I told myself, 'It will be interesting to see how this plays out.' By being open to the outcome, the vision was able to play itself out without me interfering."

Susie remarked confidently, "At the end of the day, I'm still really happy with my choices, even though they're scary."

When venturing into uncharted waters, you never know what you're going to get—clear, blue, sunny skies or stormy weather—but without some element of risk or discomfort, there's no potential for adventure—for *real* living.

Where in your life are you playing it safe? Is it in your work, your relationships, or your creative endeavors? Consider the risk of living an unfulfilled life, not living up to your highest potential, not realizing your dreams or fulfilling your purpose. Isn't this cost too great? You only have one chance in this lifetime. Why not make the most of it by taking risks now? Don't wait until it's too late!

Exercises

1. What are your limiting beliefs? Do they keep you stuck and prevent you from moving forward? Journal and explain. Look at the different areas of your life, such as finances, health, relationships, and career, and create a list of your limiting beliefs in each area. Next to each of those limiting beliefs on the page, create an affirmation or new belief you would like to replace it with. Choose your top three and write them on three-by-five-inch note cards. Place them where you can see them regularly to help you in rewiring your brain.

2. Write down the costs and benefits of taking action on a particular dream. What is a specific step you might take to move forward? Now list what is stopping you, including all of your reasons and excuses. What will you have to give up, face, or change? What will you be risking (failure, looking foolish, or facing a life without . . .)? What are your deepest fears? Are you ready to face the risks, irrational though they may be, and move ahead with this idea? Journal and explain.

3. Examine your relationships. In what ways are you playing it safe? Do you have feelings or sentiments that have gone unexpressed? If so, talk to that person. What do you have to lose? If your fears

keep you from expressing yourself face-to-face, try journaling or writing a letter first.

4. Do you feel worthy of attaining your deepest dreams and desires? If not, what can you do to love and honor yourself more? Begin a "self-honoring journal" and keep track of all the nice things you do for yourself every day. Take yourself on a "special date" once a week. Create "me time" in your schedule every day to do something you love.

5. Are you living up to your fullest potential? In what ways are you playing it safe? Explain. Create an action step that moves you beyond your comfort zone and notice how you feel.

Guided Meditation

The purpose of this meditation is to help you gain clarity about what is keeping you from moving forward, and to transform the energy of your limiting beliefs and fears so you can experience abundance.

Sit comfortably in a chair or cross-legged on a cushion on the floor with your back upright and your hands resting on your lap. Begin by bringing your focus of awareness inside to the core of your being. Notice your breath and allow it to deepen with each inhalation. Create a rhythmic flow by equally spacing your in-breath and out-breath. As you begin to relax, notice any areas in your body that feel tense or uncomfortable, and send breath to them, allowing the tension to soften and release. Next, notice the quality of your thoughts. Attempt to still your mind as you sit peacefully in silent awareness.

Take a moment to imagine your worst fear. Is it being vulnerable in relationships, taking a step toward your dreams, quitting your job, or being fully in your power and light? Do you fear being successful, failing, being judged, or dying? Once you have a clear vision of your deepest fear, take a deep breath and scan the inside of your body. Where does your fear reside? Is it in your throat, head, neck, shoulders, or stomach? Notice any place where you feel tension, discomfort, constriction, or unusual sensations. Focus your attention on this place. What does it feel like? Does it have a size, shape, or color? Develop a detailed picture of it. Then give it a name. What would you call it? Now ask this object to speak to you. Why is it here? What does it want or need? Listen closely. Does it have any messages for you?

Visualize a beam of warm golden light shining directly on this area, surrounding it with love and compassion. Picture this radiant light softening your fear, transforming it into love, freeing you from any feelings of limitation. Take a few moments to allow for the transformation to be complete. Then, notice if the object has changed shape or form. Has the color or size changed? Has it softened or shrunk? Check in with it again. Is there still something it needs in order to be transformed? Does it have any more messages for you? Allow your inner wisdom to speak to you. Sit quietly and listen.

Imagine yourself moving beyond your limiting beliefs and fears. What are you doing? Create a detailed picture of your life free from lack or limitation. Experience the joy of living up to your fullest potential and realizing your dreams. You are worthy of receiving abundance. You are whole and perfect just the way you are!

When you feel complete, slowly and gently bring yourself back to the room and open your eyes. Record your experience and any new insights that occurred to you. Try this meditation when feeling stuck or afraid of moving forward.

PART IV

THE JOURNEY

STEP 5

SWIM WITH THE DOLPHINS

» Be in Community

Never doubt that a small group of thoughtful,
committed citizens can change the world.
Indeed it is the only thing that ever has.

—MARGARET MEAD

*A*ugust 6, 1998. It is the last day of a week spent volunteering *at an elementary school in Leutoka, Fiji, while a new engine was installed in the boat. The teachers surprised me with a farewell tea, during which they presented me with a gift, a Sulu skirt, and prayed for my journey. Touched by their warmth and generosity, I felt honored, loved, and appreciated. After saying goodbye, I walked slowly away from the school, trying to savor the moment while the children ran along the fence and yelled, "Goodbye! We love you, Mrs. Karen." My heart overflowed with gratitude, and tears of joy spilled down my face.*

Experience Belonging

One of our soul's deepest longings is to feel that we are loved and that we belong. We thirst for meaningful connections, to be around and be supported by people who accept and appreciate us for who we are. Social by nature, like dolphins, we require companionship and friendship. We need to be with people with whom we can share our life experiences, dreams, and desires, and with whom we can work and play.

Studies show that we are spending more time isolated at home and are less social than ever; we are becoming increasingly disconnected from family, friends, and neighbors. Further, psychiatric disorders, including major depression and related conditions, have nearly doubled since the early 1980s. Depression now afflicts about 10 percent of adults in the United States each year. Robert

D. Putnam, the author of *Bowling Alone* and *Better Together*, commented in an interview, "Social isolation is as big a risk factor for death as smoking." He also said, "By far the strongest component of happiness is how connected you are." His conclusions are based on statistical data gathered during extensive research.

Being connected in supportive relationships not only increases our life satisfaction, it has also been found to heal us physically and emotionally while preventing isolation and loneliness, two major factors in depressive illness. In *Creating Optimism*, Bob Murray, PhD, and Alicia Fortinberry discuss techniques for building a supportive and healing network of relationships, which is, they say, "the only lasting solution to depression."

We need only look at dolphins as an example of the benefits of being connected and living in community. The love and joy they exude when working and playing together is transforming just to witness. The following story is an illustration.

We were sailing outside of Ventura Harbor in Southern California. It was mid-November and unusually warm, with blue, sunny skies and a full view of the Channel Islands. There were five of us on board: the owner and captain, a crewman, myself, and two workshop participants. The workshop was on living with passion and purpose. As if on cue, we noticed whitewater splashes in the distance, stretching over a mile. Curious, we slowly motored over to see what the commotion was about. Hundreds and hundreds of dolphins were joyfully leaping, spinning, and dancing, as if in a choreographed ballet. With what appeared to be telepathic communication, they were completely in tune with each other, synchronizing their moves to swim in unison.

Pod after pod of ten to twelve dolphins took turns approaching the boat to ride and play on the bow. While eagerly draping our hands and feet over the edge trying to touch these magnificent creatures, we could hear them singing with their sonar whistles. Like little kids at Christmas, we felt our hearts overflow with joy. This experience was the highlight of the workshop and a memory we would continue to share with others for months afterward.

Like the dolphins, we need to create human pods by developing meaningful connections and getting involved with our communities. This will allow us all to experience belonging and thus great joy and purpose in our lives.

Create a Common Purpose

The dolphins, through their pod communities, teach us about cooperation and working together in unison— each one is an integral part of the whole. They hunt fish, protect each other from predators, mate, and raise their young together, and are stronger for it. By pooling our unique gifts, we are very powerful and have the opportunity to effect positive change much more than we can alone. But in order to do so, we need to create a common purpose and work cooperatively with one another. This can be accomplished through community.

What is community? Community is a unified body of individuals brought together by common interests. There are many examples of communities in human society, including neighborhoods, jobs, social and spiritual organizations, and sports teams. While cruising from Fiji to Singapore, I felt a strong sense of community with the other sailors. We shared not only a common interest in sailing, but also a spirit of adventure. We were in it together, so we reached out for friendship and support.

Another example from my life is a community organization I participate in called EarthHEAL (Human Earth Alliance for Life). An informal group of people gathers once a month on the new moon to socialize, share ideas about healing, and honor the earth through ceremony. The people who participate have a common purpose—to heal the earth and create a sustainable planet for our future. The following story is an example of community living in which individuals work together for a different common purpose—simply to live.

While anchored off the island Waya in Fiji, John and I went ashore to explore. We had heard rumors of a village on the other side of the island, and our curiosity prodded us to continue on despite feeling tired and hungry after having hiked over two hours in unbearable heat.

Descending toward a cove on the trail, it was quiet except for the faint sound of music. Small hut-style houses began appearing as the music got louder and louder. Finally, to our surprise, we came upon a group of about two hundred Fijian natives gathered. The older men were in front, conducting a ceremony, while the middle-aged men and women performed a dance in the middle. On the outskirts, the older women and children sat observing.

Slowly, we approached, trying to be respectful, and then watched quietly in the background. Communicating with sign language and smiles, we made friends with a few of the children and were invited by the grandmothers to attend a celebration luncheon concluding the ceremony. The meal was Fijian style—we sat on the floor and ate with our hands. Rice, lamb, casaba, fruit-bread, and fish eggs were among the cuisine, which filled our hungry bellies.

During our brief glimpse into this culture, we observed how the people worked together, living mostly off the sea and land and pooling their resources to help each other in a supportive community environment. They appeared joyful and happy, smiling frequently with a twinkle in their eyes. Even though they had so little materially, they were rich in emotion and spirit.

Due to our modern lives, we no longer live in supportive community environments like this, and so we need to find ways to be in community with each other. When choosing a community to be involved with, consider what your interests and passions are. What do you feel strongly about? Put your energy where your passion is and surround yourself with positive, supportive, like-minded people with whom your heart resonates.

Honor One Another's Uniqueness

When in community, it is important to honor one another's unique gifts and differences. Tolerance and acceptance of group members, as well as other communities with differing viewpoints, is critical. A community ought to foster unity and make the lives of its members and the surrounding communities even better.

Too often, we fear what we don't understand and adopt defenses such as judgment to make ourselves feel better—safer. Judgment only breeds intolerance, hatred, and violence, hurting everyone involved. When we are judgmental, even our thoughts are destructive, because they transmit negative energy. They project an attitude of being "better than," making it unsafe for the other person to be themselves. Since we have never walked in the other person's shoes, how can we possibly know what they are going through and experiencing? We are all doing our very best with the knowledge and wisdom we have. So instead of criticizing and judging, develop love, tolerance, and compassion.

When we keep an open mind toward diverse ways of thinking, believing, and living, our own consciousness expands, creating opportunities to live more fully and adding richness and beauty to our existence. For example, while you are traveling, honor the differing traditions and customs of the cultures you visit. Learn from them. Why do they do things the way they do? What do their traditions mean to them? In the Muslim countries John and I visited, the people gathered to pray several times a day, beginning early in the morning. From the sailboat, we could hear bells ringing to notify the community of prayer time. When this happened, I appreciated the reminder to take time out and honor my own spiritual connection.

While honoring our differences, we also need to take the time to *really* get to know one another. Since ignorance causes judgment, educate yourself about the other person's thoughts, feelings, and beliefs. What are their deepest dreams and desires? What do they value most? Tolerance and compassion grow when we try to understand exactly where others are coming from. Also, focus on your similarities instead of your differences. As human beings, we all share the same core need and desire—to love and be loved—and we all experience pain and suffering. Maybe you and the other person share similar trials—the loss of a loved one or a serious health condition, for instance. Find out what you have in common. Go further, and see beyond your differences to the unique gifts the other person has to offer. In *The Shelter of Each Other*, Mary Pipher, PhD, suggests:

> A new cultural definition of wealth could be not the GNP, but how many people truly know and care about each other. This definition of cultural wealth is related to Margaret Mead's definition of an ideal human culture, as one in which there is a place for every human gift. It is hard to realize the gifts of people whom we do not know. In an ideal culture people know each other enough to acknowledge and support each other in the development of their individual gifts.

Take time to reach out and get to know the people in your neighborhood and your community—*really* know them. Look for the unique gifts each person has to offer, and develop tolerance and compassion. By honoring the individuals in your community, you are contributing to global peace. But first you must develop love and harmony within yourself. There is a saying by Confucius that goes:

> When there is light in the soul, there is beauty in the person.
> When there is beauty in the person, there is harmony within the home.

When there is harmony within the home, there is order in the nation.
When there is order in the nation, there is peace in the world.

Peace begins by dissolving judgment—judgments about ourselves and others. In what ways have you closed your mind to others' ways of living? Take a moment and examine your thoughts, attitudes, and beliefs. Do you think your way of living and doing things is the best or only way? How does this belief create division or separation? Since each of us is a unique expression of the Divine, created in perfection to serve a special purpose, why would we dishonor or judge anyone, including ourselves?

If you find you are having trouble letting go of judgmental thoughts or attitudes, visualize sending love to this person or group of people. Attempt to put yourself in their shoes. This will assist with opening your mind and heart. Also, take time to get to know them. How are they special? How are their differences a gift? By supporting others to be their best and accepting them for who they are, you are creating a consciousness of love and unity, which will lead to a more fulfilling life and a more harmonious world.

Develop Meaningful Connections

Meaningful connections based on mutual sharing, caring, respect, trust, understanding, and love can be made with anyone with whom you share heart to heart, including family members, romantic partners, work colleagues, and friends. They can even be with people you meet in passing at the grocery store, during a party, or while walking on the beach. The connection can be a glance or smile from a stranger that uplifts you, a five-minute conversation that touches you deeply, or a lifetime relationship. Being present to receive the gift of the connection is what makes it meaningful.

In order to develop meaningful connections, we need to be willing to take the time to communicate openly and honestly; to share our deepest dreams and desires, our fears and disappointments; and to spend quality time together working, playing, and growing. By mutually sharing of ourselves—our thoughts, feelings, and wisdom—we have the opportunity to develop. Not only do we learn from one another's knowledge and experiences, but the people we are close to act as mirrors, reflecting aspects of ourselves and teaching us where we need to grow. For example, maybe you are bothered when others give you unsolicited advice but, upon reflection, you see this behavior in yourself. When feeling angry, frustrated, or irritated with someone, ask what they may be reflecting. What can you learn from them? Our close connections also reflect our strengths and talents. Sometimes it is easier for someone else to see our unique gifts and positive qualities than it is for us to see them.

Like a beautiful garden, meaningful relationships take time, energy, and attention to cultivate. The seeds need to be planted, watered, and fertilized, and the soil tilled, for the flowers to blossom, just as your connections need to be nurtured, prioritized, and honored. You can do this by giving your time and undivided attention to the other person—by listening, *really* listening and being present with your entire being, your body, mind, and soul. It can be easy to take the other for granted, thinking they will always be there, or to only half-listen when they are talking to us, our mind on a hundred other things.

The next time you are in a conversation, practice being totally present. Tune out all other distractions and focus on hearing what is being said. Listen with all of your senses, including your ears, eyes, and heart, as the other person may be communicating something much deeper than the words being spoken. Also, demonstrate that you are really listening by asking questions about what is being said. Being totally present during your conversations is one of the greatest gestures of love you can offer.

If you find you are frequently self-absorbed and are taking your connections for granted, try sending a card to a friend or writing a love letter to your partner. Do something special, unexpected, thoughtful, generous, and creative. If you live in another city, connect with a "circle journal." Write what you are thinking, feeling, and experiencing in a small journal. Include pictures or mementos and mail it to your friend, who will then respond in kind. Keep the journal circulating between you.

To build intimacy, spend more *quality* time with your partner or friend. Consider scheduling a date just to sit and talk, or to go out and have fun. If you have kids, hire a babysitter once a week so you and your partner can focus on each other without distractions. It is worth the extra effort to make your important relationships a priority.

Quality connections have the ability to bring out the best in us. But first we must know and love ourselves— be our own best friend. If we lack self-love, we will expect the other person to build us up, love us, and fulfill us, creating a needy attachment rather than a mutually supportive and loving relationship. By coming together from a place of wholeness and strength, not neediness, we have so much more to offer. The relationship has a healthy basis on which to stand and can therefore support us to reach our potential. But the opposite is true if the connection is built on neediness. The relationship will be dysfunctional, causing pain while depleting our life-force energy.

How do you approach your relationships? Is it from a place of need and lack, or one of empowerment? If you find yourself frequently feeling insecure, jealous, possessive, or controlling, then you may need to work on improving your self-esteem. Consider finding a good therapist to assist you with the process.

Our connections can be a few or many, as we all have differing social needs. Some people are extroverted and get their energy by being around other people, while others are introverted and need to restore their energy by being alone. In many cases, one or two close relationships are sufficient. Quality, not quantity, is the key.

If you are introverted and prefer spending time alone, or if you have trouble getting out of the house for physical reasons, then consider getting a pet to fulfill your needs for companionship, love, and affection. But remember, an animal cannot provide *all* of your social needs.

Maybe you are shy and feel lonely and have trouble developing meaningful connections. If this is the case, consider getting involved in activities where you can meet people with common interests, such as a skiing or boating club or your church's social events. Reach out and be assertive. Get to know individuals by asking questions about their lives and *really* listening. If they respond with questions about you, then the interest is mutual, so feel free to ask them to meet for lunch or coffee. Be willing to openly share your life stories. Over time, you will build trust and respect—the seeds of a fulfilling relationship.

Living a purposeful life requires that we take the time to till the soil of intimacy and develop connections by giving of ourselves while receiving the gift of the other.

Choose to Get Involved

Get involved in what you love and feel passionate about, what will bring you joy and fulfillment. Whether it's a church group, social club, sports team, or other organization, put yourself out there with other people, where you have the opportunity to develop meaningful connections.

Carol, a seventy-two-year-old widow, joined a senior citizens' organization after her husband died. She keeps busy with social activities and travels frequently with people with whom she has common interests, and she has made many new friends. She also helps out with her grandchildren—dropping them off and picking them up at school—and helps care for a blind friend. She has chosen to reach out, meet new people, and experience life rather than cut herself off from friends and family. As a result, her life is more enjoyable and fulfilling.

We have a fundamental need not only to connect with others, but also to feel useful, like we are making a positive difference. Don, who is sixty-five and recently retired, spends time once a week volunteering in his daughter's classroom. She is a sixth-grade teacher of special-needs students. He typically helps with reading and math and sees himself as a "role model and father figure." Don shared, "Some of these kids don't have healthy role models, so it's extremely rewarding to be there for them."

After selling his company, Don still spends time at work mentoring the business's new owners and employees. He enjoys sharing his knowledge and experience with younger people and giving them advice when it is sought.

He also participates on the design committee in his housing community, where he is able to offer his expertise as a contractor. He said, "It's important to be involved with something outside of work where you can give of yourself, participate, and learn something new."

Don finds working with the other committee members to be very rewarding. He's been able to meet people with common interests, "which has opened the possibility for developing future friendships," he said.

By reaching out and getting involved, Don's life is very meaningful.

Gina, a fifty-one-year-old psychotherapist and mother, is very involved in her community and participates in several different organizations. One in particular is "the Circle," a spiritually focused group that began gathering in 1990 to socialize, support each other, and meditate.

"You get so distracted by everyday life. This has been a very centering experience, bringing you back to who you really are," Gina explained.

"It's really sustained a lot of people," she added. "It became clear that each person had a unique gift that benefited everyone and catapulted the group to a new level of growth and understanding. There always appeared to be a purpose in our gatherings, like we were a part of something larger."

Over time, a common purpose developed for the Circle: to understand the sacred reciprocity of humans and the earth, and to do whatever possible to create a sustainable future. The group became concerned by a six-year drought, which exacerbated an infestation of bark beetles killing the trees in the San Bernardino Mountains of Southern California. Consequently, the members approached a Native American Eastern Shoshone elder who had knowledge and experience of earth-healing practices, and they developed a ceremony referred to as the Big Bear Medicine Wheel. Big Bear was the hub of the wheel, with spokes reaching out to eight sacred sites in a 120-mile radius. The ceremony expressed love and gratitude for the earth while setting intentions for healing.

Given the amount of preparation needed, the group divided responsibilities according to each member's strengths. Group members chose ambassadors for each site, sent out communication to invite participation, raised funds, and conducted training. After the training, the first ceremony was performed. Excitedly, Gina shared, "A little rain was expected, and we received two feet of snow that night. The ski slopes opened a month early!"

The Medicine Wheel ceremony took place about three weeks later and concluded with a final celebration to honor the participants. That night, a "dusting" of snow was predicted, but it snowed three feet over the next few days. Gina exclaimed, "The weather forecasters were baffled!" Needless to say, the ceremony was a success. Two years later, the lakes are still full.

"The group now sees itself as stewards of the land," said Gina. The members will continue to work together to do what they can to create a sustainable future for our planet, including teaching children to live in harmony with nature.

Gina shared advice about getting involved: "First, figure out what it is you desire. The organization needs to be in alignment with your interests and intentions."

Next, she said, "Take time to learn what the group is about before joining. Attend several meetings and feel it out. Is the intention clear, or is the group mired in personality differences, petty conflicts, and power struggles?"

Finally, she added, "People need people. Women definitely need women, because they can get caught up in the caretaker role and lose a sense of purpose apart from that role. Women need the wisdom and nurturing of other women, because sometimes they nurture others to the point of running out of energy themselves."

When we gather together in community, we have the opportunity to receive love and support while making a contribution with our unique gifts and working toward a common purpose. As a result, our involvement increases our vital life-force energy and our experience of love and joy.

If you feel uncomfortable participating in community by yourself, then invite a friend to come along. It can be scary to join something on your own, that is, until you get acquainted with the people involved. Also, if you feel you are too busy, begin with activities that take a minimal amount of time and focus on things you love to do and that bring you joy.

One step at a time, one connection at a time, your life will become more fulfilling and the world will be a better place.

Exercises

1. Do you feel a sense of belonging in your life? If not, evaluate your social network. Make a list of family members, friends, romantic partners, acquaintances, neighbors, and work colleagues. Are there gaping

holes in your list? If so, what type of relationships would you like to manifest in your life? Make your intentions known by writing down the qualities of the person or people you would like to attract.

2. Do you feel a sense of community in your life, where you are working with others toward a common purpose? If not, how can you develop this? Journal and explain.

3. Observe your thoughts, attitudes, beliefs, and behaviors. Are you supporting others to be their best? Are you accepting them for who they are? If you have judgmental thoughts, take the time to really understand the other person. Attempt to put yourself in their shoes, and visualize sending love their way.

4. How do you feel about the quality of your connections with people? Do you desire deeper relationships? Explain. Take time out of your busy schedule and set a date to go out, have fun, talk, be present, and listen. Ask about the other person's deepest dreams and desires. What are their thoughts, feelings, and attitudes about life? What are their disappointments?

5. What are your passions and interests? Are there organizations in your community that you can get involved in to meet like-minded people? If not, can

you start one? What about making a contribution by volunteering your time? Begin by taking small steps to reach out. For example, talk to a neighbor, go on a picnic with a friend, attend a meeting of a group you would like to participate in, or research volunteer opportunities.

Guided Meditation

This meditation will assist you in experiencing the love and joy of being a part of something larger than yourself.

Sit comfortably in a chair or cross-legged on a cushion on the floor with your back upright and your hands resting on your lap. Begin by bringing your focus of awareness inside to the core of your being. Notice your breath and allow it to deepen with each inhalation. Create a rhythmic flow by equally spacing your in-breath and out-breath. As you begin to relax, notice any areas in your body that feel tense or uncomfortable, and send breath to them, allowing the tension to soften and release. Next, notice the quality of your thoughts. Attempt to still your mind as you sit peacefully in silent awareness.

Imagine you are swimming in the warm, aqua blue water of the tropics. The waves are small and gentle, allowing you to glide along the water with ease. In the distance, you glimpse a pod of dolphins, and you decide to swim over and join them. They are delighted by your presence and greet you warmly by carefully nuzzling up against you. Love and joy emanate from their eyes. Welcoming you into their pod, you feel accepted, loved, and honored—a part of something very special.

As you swim with the dolphins, imagine being surrounded by your loved ones too, whether that is your family, friends, partner, or pets. Your loved ones join you to create a human pod, like the dolphins do. As part of this pod, you feel a deep sense of love and belonging.

Visualize your pod connecting with other human pods and communities, creating a web of light and love. Watch as these connections multiply to include your neighborhood, community, city, state, country, and continent, until the web expands around the entire world. Take a moment to allow yourself to feel your connection to all other beings. You are one.

Allow the energy of the ocean water and the love of the dolphins to cleanse you of any judgments you may have toward yourself and others. As your judgments wash away, love and compassion fill your heart. Experience the freedom of being in a place of honoring all beings for their unique contribution to the web.

When you feel complete, slowly and gently bring yourself back to the room and open your eyes. Record your experience and any new insights that occurred to you. What can you do to create a greater sense of belonging and community in your life?

STEP 6

CONNECT INTIMATELY WITH ALL LIFE

» *Slow Down*

Those who contemplate the beauty of the earth find reserves of strength that will endure as long as life lasts.

—Rachel Carson

September 6, 1998. We are on passage to Australia, it's about 6:30 p.m., and we just finished dinner. The sun's flaming orange brilliance catches our attention as she goes down for the night. While she descends, we notice a large yellow harvest moon rising on our stern, amidst the watercolors of the sunset's residue. I do not know which way to look—west at the orange hues covering miles of the horizon, or east at the river of gold trailing our boat. This is the perfect cruising night. I am totally relaxed and at peace with the world. Nature is in harmony, and my soul sings in ecstasy.

Experience Sacredness

In our modern, fast-paced society, many of us live in our heads. We feel isolated, disconnected—from life, our own souls, God, the earth, and each other. The fast pace we live at is a result of the vicious cycle of consumerism. We purchase things we don't really need or rarely use, such as large houses with unused rooms and toys we don't have time for. To pay for all of this, we stay busy earning an income, leaving us with little time to really connect on a deep, intimate level. We may attend church once a week and experience a brief spiritual connection, or we may occasionally spend time in nature. But when engaging in these activities, how present are we? Are we connecting deeply, experiencing the sacredness of the moment?

In the movie *Captain Ron*, starring Kurt Russell, Martin Short finds out that he has inherited his uncle's sailing yacht. Excited, he proposes to his wife that they take off for "an adventure of a lifetime." Her response is, "We'll be spontaneous when we have time." She wants to sell the boat to pay off their second mortgage and credit cards. This is the perfect example of how our overconsuming creates a situation in which we are too busy paying our bills to be spontaneous and enjoy life.

Living on automatic pilot, just trying to make it through the day, we have forgotten that we have choices. We *can* control the speed of the treadmill—or choose to get off altogether to walk at our own pace and take breaks along the way.

In the movie, Martin Short finally convinces his wife to take a break from their harried lives in order to deliver his uncle's boat to the mainland. Although their cruising adventure is a joke, with one mishap after another, they ultimately come together and thoroughly enjoy themselves. In the final scene, as they return home and sail into the harbor, feeling empowered, they decide at the last minute to turn around, keep cruising, and leave their old, frenzied life behind.

If we continue running on the treadmill, feeling unempowered, stressed, and unfulfilled—less than vibrant—then our bodies will eventually break down and force us to stop. What we need now more than ever is to slow down so that we can connect deeply with all life and experience the beauty and sacredness surrounding us, before it's too late. One way we can do this is by spending quality time in nature and being present with all our senses. By consciously connecting to nature—the very thing that enlivens, nourishes, feeds, and sustains us—we will begin to wake up and see the consequences of our actions. Our habit of overconsuming is depleting our natural resources and destroying our planet, our home. When we see what we are doing to our source of life, we can choose to make positive changes that will simplify our lifestyles.

An intimate connection with all life begins with connecting to ourselves. By listening to our bodies—our own nature—and connecting to our higher guidance for wisdom and clarity, we learn that what we *really* need to be satisfied is already within us. There is nothing outside of ourselves that can offer us lasting satisfaction.

We also need to take time out from the routine of our lives to re-evaluate where we are and where we are heading, to recharge our batteries, and to honor ourselves, celebrate our accomplishments, and mark the transitions in our lives. Too often, we don't stop to appreciate where we have been before we move on.

Taking the time to slow down and connect intimately with all life, we are better able to experience living in the moment—in the now. In *Stillness Speaks*, Eckhart Tolle wrote, "The more you live in the Now, the more you sense the simple yet profound joy of Being and the sacredness of all life." Living in the now requires that we be grounded in our bodies and listen to our hearts instead of the constant chatter of our busy minds. From our hearts, we can experience the mystery of our interconnection with all life, and we are able to experience great joy and purpose.

Connect with Your Inner Wisdom

To know ourselves intimately, we need to listen to our inner wisdom—the wisdom of our bodies, hearts, and spirits. This inner wisdom guides us to act in our highest good and make decisions that are in alignment with who we are and our deepest desires. When we connect with our inner wisdom, we need to trust what we are hearing and act accordingly. If we dismiss what we are hearing, we may cause ourselves unnecessary suffering. For example, have you ever had an intuitive hunch or feeling about something and not followed it? Maybe you felt tired and your body was telling you to rest, but then you pushed it and got sick as a result. Our lives unfold with divine perfection as we listen to, trust, and act on our inner wisdom.

One way to connect with your inner wisdom is to sit quietly and listen to your body. Through symptoms of pain and illness, our bodies reveal messages about where we are out of balance and give us information about our emotional state. For example, a headache may be your body's way of communicating that you feel unsafe or insecure. A cold may be telling you to slow down, that you have too much going on, and that you're feeling overwhelmed. In *You Can Heal Your Life*, Louise L. Hay wrote, "The body, like everything else in life, is a mirror of our inner thoughts and beliefs. The body is always talking to us, if we will only take the time to listen. Every cell within your body responds to every single thought you think and every word you speak." By slowing down and listening to your body, your awareness will expand and your life will transform.

We also need to listen to our hearts and spirits as they speak to us about our passions, dreams, and desires. Your heart and spirit communicate who you are—your gifts, likes, dislikes, and needs—and help you gain clarity about your life's direction and purpose. As you sit quietly and listen to your heart, notice what brings a smile to your face, makes you feel warm and cozy, stirs your passions, and inspires your creativity. Pay attention to what opens your heart and nourishes your soul. Does a certain relationship or environment uplift and inspire you? Maybe your heart opens while being surrounded by nature, or maybe when in the middle of a city, surrounded by people with diverse cultural backgrounds. Each one of us has unique passions and desires, so listen to and follow your own heart, and trust it to lead you to a more purposeful life.

In establishing a strong relationship with ourselves, it's important that we connect on a daily basis. I call it *checking in* or *getting centered*. There are so many distractions in life caused by our relationships or unexpected stressors that it is easy to get blown off course. For example, your partner might come home in a bad mood, therefore putting you in a negative place. Or your child might get sick, causing you to stay home from work and get behind schedule on a project. By strengthening your inner connection through a daily routine, you will be able to make more empowered decisions from a centered place. Your partner's mood won't affect you, and your child's illness won't cause you to stress out. You will feel more peace, strength, and clarity and will be able to go out into the world with purpose and direction—to navigate your own journey, as opposed to living your life in reaction to the things happening around you.

In addition, when you take time to be present with yourself, you allow room for processing your feelings and experiences. So often, we go throughout our day from one activity to the next and ignore what we are experiencing. If we check in, we can get in touch with these feelings and process them instead of repressing them in our bodies until they eventually come out through illness or outbursts of anger.

Robin, a forty-eight-year-old psychologist, teaches her clients "essential centering" skills to decrease stress and increase relaxation, balance, rejuvenation, and their own natural healing responses. "When stress builds up, the slightest thing can trigger a total meltdown. Anger, crying, shouting, drama—scenes at the post office or grocery store," Robin explained.

"It's important to learn how to relax, but it takes practice, lots of practice. It's hard work," she added. Therefore, it is important to develop a daily routine that feels comfortable and works for you.

There are many ways to regain balance, get centered, and connect with your inner wisdom—working out, spending time in nature, meditating, praying, journaling, practicing yoga, going to church, or talking with a therapist or like-minded friend. When developing your practice, experiment with different modalities until you find what works best for you.

Meditation is one technique that has been found to help with finding relaxation, balancing emotions, and shutting out the chatter of our busy minds. Besides helping us connect with our inner wisdom, meditation also has physical benefits, such as lowering blood pressure. The following is an example of how to get started:

Find a place where you won't be interrupted, like a quiet room in your house or a spot in nature—on top of a hill, under a tree, or by a creek. Sit in a comfortable position with your spine straight. Close your eyes and begin focusing on your breath. As you follow the sensation of your breath, notice the quality of your mind. Are your thoughts racing? Are they positive or negative? Don't judge what you observe, just bring your awareness to it. Focusing in this way will help stabilize your attention, keeping you mindful and alert. If you feel uncomfortable, leave the breath for a while and widen your focus of attention by noticing what you observe with your senses, like sounds appearing and disappearing or sensations in your body. As you practice, your mind will eventually quiet down and you will notice the space between your thoughts. Allow this space to expand as you sit in silent awareness.

Begin by sitting still for five minutes at a time. As you feel comfortable, expand the amount of time you spend or increase how often you meditate. For example, instead of once a day, do two short meditations. You can also meditate briefly while you take a break at work, sitting quietly in your car, in your office with the door closed, or in a nearby park. As you close your eyes, focus on your breath. With each exhalation, release the tension from your day and relax. Connect with your inner wisdom and listen. What is your body communicating to you? What are the desires of your heart? Try asking yourself a yes/no question, and listen to what emerges. As you practice taking time out to check in and get centered, notice how you feel. Do you feel more balanced, clear, and calm?

From stillness and silence, we are able to connect to our infinite Source of love, joy, peace, and wisdom. Answers emerge from the dark, lighting our path. We are able to get in touch with the deepest parts of ourselves, the places that need healing, our fears and our light. Creating silence and stillness in our chaotic, busy lives is essential to living a purposeful life.

The following is an example of a twenty-minute daily routine to still your mind and check in with yourself:

- Journal for ten minutes every morning, writing about your thoughts, feelings, and experiences. Process an event or conversation that is bothering you. Journal about the dreams you had last night. Include your intentions for the day and all that you are grateful for. Write fast and from your heart, releasing anything on your mind.

- Pray and meditate for ten minutes after journaling. Spend time visualizing your desires, expressing gratitude for what has already shown up in your life, asking for guidance, and listening. Slow your thoughts and *really* listen.

- Before going to sleep at night, create an intention for what you wish to happen, such as, "I desire more guidance on an article I'm writing," "I wish to sleep soundly and feel rested when I awaken," or "I want for this pain to be healed." By setting your intentions before going to sleep, you are allowing the Universe to assist you through your subconscious mind.

- Wake up the next morning and start all over again with journaling.

If you find yourself thinking, "This sounds great, but I don't have the time," consider the fact that you might actually be saving time. For example, when you are in a centered and connected place, things flow more smoothly. You are guided to the best actions, resources show up unexpectedly to assist you, and you complete your tasks with ease and grace.

As you make a commitment to getting centered and checking in with your inner wisdom on a daily basis, you will gain clarity about your life's purpose and direction, you will experience more love and peace, and your life will transform.

Spend Quality Time in Nature

One way we can connect more deeply with ourselves is to spend quality time in nature. Because we are surrounded by concrete and boxed in by houses, cars, and offices, most of us have lost this vital connection. When we do spend time outdoors, how often do we slow down enough to be fully present with all of our senses—studying the intricacies of a flower or butterfly, really listening to the birds sing or the wind rustle through the leaves of a tree, smelling freshly cut grass, or sticking our toes in the cool running water of an alpine creek? By taking the time to connect intimately with nature, we become aware of the inner connection of all living things and are brought back to what is essential. Our worldly worries vanish, and we have the opportunity to experience great joy, abundance, and vitality.

While hiking the other day, I consciously slowed down to connect with nature. I noticed how busy the bugs, beetles, and butterflies were and how the stream of water flowed effortlessly down the mountain with direction and purpose, following the path of least resistance while nourishing life along the way. The plants, birds, and trees were all at home in their environment, living out their unique purpose without doubt or hesitation, doing what came naturally, following life's cycles and seasons, all performing a function.

The butterflies taught me about beauty, lightness of being, and grace, about the importance of going through our own metamorphosis and transformation before we can spread our wings and fly. Each one had its own unique beauty—all differing sizes, shapes, and colors. They reminded me of our own uniqueness, and of the imagination of our wonderful Creator. As the clear mountain water washed over them, the stones I saw also displayed a diversity of colors—orange, red, green, and purple—and the beautiful wildflowers were indigo, violet, yellow, orange, pink, and white.

By slowing down and taking the time to be present, I felt immersed in this web of life, connected to the life force of all living things. The trees, bugs, animals, and rocks all have life force at differing levels of density and awareness. As I became absorbed in the vibrant life and consciousness surrounding me, I felt totally alive. My heart was open and full of gratitude for nature's wisdom, beauty, and grace, and for all of her lessons.

Diane, a forty-five-year-old mother and waitress, loves to run. She has recently become more aware of her vital connection to the earth, and instead of running on concrete sidewalks and streets, she has been running on mountain trails. Enthusiastically, she shared, "I don't want to come inside after I run. I wish I could live in a teepee so I could be outside all the time." Being in nature enlivens her spirit, causing her to feel vigorous and alive.

Since Diane is unable to live outside full time, she does what she can to bring nature inside her house. "My house is full of plants, rocks, seashells, and even sand," she said. During her last trip to the beach, she brought sand home in a box so she could put her feet in it.

Diane said emphatically, "Nature is never too busy. It doesn't say 'Oh, tomorrow' or 'Later.' It has all the time in the world. It's you who has to slow down and make the time."

As you slow down and spend quality moments in nature, practice being still and silent. Listen to your inner wisdom. Are there lessons or messages being communicated to you? What can you learn by observing nature? Notice her divine perfection in the amazing design of a flower or starfish. As part of nature, you too are beautiful, perfect, and complete—just the way you are. You have abundant wealth within you and do not need to search for it outside of yourself. Being who you are is enough.

What is your relationship with nature? Is it close and intimate, like a best friend, or distant, like a long-lost relative you see every few years? What can you do to strengthen this vital connection? If you live in a city, find the nearest park or beach and spend time there regularly. Take your shoes off and walk barefoot on the grass, dirt, or sand. Gaze at the stars and moon while contemplating the vastness of the Universe. Meditate on the ocean waves as they continuously build and crash.

By spending quality time in nature, you will experience balance in your life, greater vitality, and a stronger connection to your inner wisdom.

Connect to Your Source

We all have available to us an infinite Source of love and abundance. Each one of us has equal access to this flow of energy. As with a water faucet, we have the ability to control the flow—to turn the faucet on or off. It's our choice. During a hike the other day, I stopped to meditate by a beautiful, vibrant tree. The tree was growing in the path of a stream of water. Because of its constant connection to its source of life, it grew strong and healthy. Similarly, when we regularly tap into the ever-present Source of love and abundance, we flourish and experience well-being, just like the tree.

In order to access this Source of energy, it is helpful to raise our own energy vibration by increasing positive thoughts and feelings, such as love and joy. By raising our vibration, we are creating a clear channel, free from blockages, and are better able to receive abundantly.

Practicing meditation is an excellent way to increase your energy vibration and connection to Source. To prepare for meditation, try doing yoga to slow down your mind. Yoga will also assist you to regain balance and clarity, ease anxiety and depression, heal emotional wounds, and increase your sense of personal power. Journaling is another tool to prepare you for meditation by assisting you to release the chatter in your mind. Julia Cameron, author of *The Artist's Way*, suggests writing three morning pages every day. First thing in the morning, fill three journal pages with your thoughts, feelings, dreams, and experiences, writing from your heart as fast as you can. During the process, you will become aware of any blocks or fears you may be experiencing and can then create positive affirmations to begin transforming them.

The following are additional techniques to cleanse your energy, increase your vibration, and connect to your Source:

- Meditate with a group of friends on a regular basis. This is an incredibly powerful way of increasing your energy vibrations of love and joy while reaching deeper levels of awareness.

- Be mindful when taking a shower or bath, as water is a very strong energy transformer. While showering, set your intentions to cleanse yourself of any negative energy, and picture it washing down the drain. Imagine the spray of water as white light flowing through you and surrounding you. While taking a bath, use sea salts or Epsom salts. Combine these with baking soda for an even greater energy-cleansing effect, and add essential oils such as lavender, rosemary, and sage.

- Burn incense or sage to clear stagnant energy in your home or office.

- Participate in a ritual or ceremony with the intention of clearing blocks. Write on a piece of paper or blow into a stick what you want to release, and then burn it in a fire. This can be done individually or in a group. (A group ritual is more powerful, as the energy is heightened.)

- Create sacred space by lighting a candle, burning incense, playing soulful music, setting up an altar with meaningful objects, or using sound, such as ringing a bell.

- Pray, expressing gratitude to Creator for all that you are and all that is in your life. Love and gratitude are the highest forms of energy. When praying, use it as a dialogue of power, not of supplication; that is, say, "Show me what I need to see. Teach me what I need to know. Take me where I need to go."

- Tone, sing, chant, or sigh—that is, use the vibration of your own voice to move energy. As you sigh, imagine the energy starting at the top of your head, moving down through your body, and being expelled through your feet into the earth. Do this several times until you feel lighter.

- Practice deep breathing. Breathe in from your nose, sending breath all the way down into your belly to fill it up like a balloon. As you exhale, press the air out with the muscles in your abdomen. Create an equal flow between your in-breath and out-breath. Continue until you feel refreshed.

- Cultivate mindfulness during your daily routine, such as when eating, taking a shower, driving, and exercising. Write "Be Mindful" on three-by-five-inch note cards to remind you to slow down and be present. Place them around your house, near your desk, and in your car.

- Pay attention to what you eat. Avoid sugar, caffeine, nicotine, alcohol, and chocolate. Drink pure water and eat plenty of organic fresh fruits and vegetables.

- Engage in activities with movement, like dance, exercise, walking fast, qi gong, or tai chi.

- Move blocked energy with acupuncture, acupressure, chiropractic, or massage.

- Express yourself creatively through painting, drawing, or playing music.

- Listen to high-vibration music that makes you feel good.

- Surround yourself with people, places, and things that you love.

The above techniques will help you clear your energy and raise your vibration so you can tap into the ultimate Source of love and abundance. As a result, you will experience a greater sense of well-being and joy. You will also have an open channel for receiving clarity and guidance.

In a recent interview, Dan Millman, the author of *Way of the Peaceful Warrior*, was quoted as saying, "There's no lack of God or spirit or beauty or inspiration, whatever we want to call it. It's always here, but we don't always notice it." As we consciously connect to our Source, our spirits will awaken. We will notice the beauty surrounding us in our daily lives and won't take for granted the miraculous gifts that show up.

Take Time Out Regularly

We need to take time out regularly to slow down and connect. By moving away from our daily routines to meditate, reflect, and contemplate our lives, we are able to gain clarity, restore balance, and recharge our batteries. Spending time in solitude, we revitalize our supply of love and energy and are better able to give back.

Gina, the fifty-one-year-old psychotherapist mentioned earlier, recently went away to spend one week alone in silent retreat. She did not watch TV, check voice mail or e-mail, talk on the phone, read books, or even listen to music. Instead, she fasted for a couple of days to cleanse her system, spent time in deep meditation, prepared healthy organic meals, walked outdoors, and slept. She said, "I wasn't bored or lonely for one second."

Excited, she continued, "It cleared my head. I felt like I gained a lot of clarity about who I am, what I want, and what I'm willing to do." Gina returned home with a renewed sense of energy and clarity about her life. "It was the best thing I've ever done," she added.

She plans to do this every year from now on. "Some women will object that they can't take time away from their children, but my family has noticed the difference in me, and they weathered my absence just fine," Gina explained.

So, if possible, take time out to go on a retreat, where you can spend a significant amount of time in stillness and silence. If you can't afford to be gone an entire week, schedule a weekend for yourself to be away from all the responsibilities and distractions in your life.

Traveling is another form of taking time out that gets us out of our normal routine. It awakens our senses, causing us to be much more in the moment and better able to connect. Traveling to different countries especially puts us in the moment, as the sights, sounds, and smells are so unique and the culture, language, and customs so different. Schedule regular vacations to new and exciting places you have always wanted to see.

We also need to take time out to celebrate our accomplishments—a job well done, a creative endeavor completed, the birth of a new life, the purchase of a new home, the arrival at the destination of our dreams. Indigenous cultures celebrated all cycles of the seasons, including the solstices and equinoxes. Transitions in human life were also honored with ceremonies, such as when a boy or girl reached puberty. By marking the transitions in your life before moving on to the next destination, you will experience more sacredness.

Indigenous cultures can teach us about living in harmony and balance and treating life as sacred. So much of our energy is spent out there trying to make things happen—striving, competing, and working. In the process, we have lost our connection with each other, Source, the earth, and ourselves. As a result, many of us have become dissatisfied. This way of living is also destroying our planet, our home. We need to balance our doing and achieving with being still and receiving, before it's too late.

Exercises

1. Cultivate mindfulness during your daily routine, such as when eating, taking a shower, driving, or exercising. Write "Be Mindful" on note cards to

remind you to slow down and be present. Place them around your house and in your office and car.

2. Develop a daily practice to slow down and check in. Try journaling for ten minutes. Write quickly and from your heart about your thoughts, feelings, and experiences. Then meditate for ten minutes, sitting quietly and focusing on your breath. Listen to your body's wisdom. What is it trying to communicate to you? What is your heart saying? When you're done meditating, journal again and allow your inner wisdom to flow through you.

3. Set aside time in your week to be outdoors and immerse yourself in nature, even if it's only sitting in your backyard or walking down a tree-lined street. Take off your shoes and walk in the grass, sand, or dirt. Smell the flowers. Listen to the birds sing. Be fully present with all of your senses and notice how you feel.

4. Create sacred space in your home where you can pray, journal, meditate, do yoga, sing, and dance. Light a candle, burn incense, play music, and set up an altar with meaningful pictures and objects. This is your special place to connect. Visit it frequently.

5. Schedule time alone for a silent retreat, whether it's for one day, a weekend, or a week. Turn off your phone, pager, computer, and television. Fast for one

or two days, and then eat only unprocessed organic foods. Be totally present with yourself, and spend time journaling, meditating, walking outdoors, and sleeping. Notice how you feel. Do you have more energy and clarity? Do this at least once a year.

Guided Meditation

This meditation is designed to assist you in connecting below (earth), above (Source), within, and without— through the heart, through love.

Sit comfortably in a chair with your feet on the floor and your back upright. Begin by bringing your focus of awareness inside to the core of your being. Notice your breath and allow it to deepen with each inhalation. Create a rhythmic flow by equally spacing your in-breath and out-breath. As you begin to relax, notice any areas in your body that feel tense or uncomfortable, and send breath to them, allowing the tension to soften and release. Next, notice the quality of your thoughts. Attempt to still your mind as you sit peacefully in silent awareness.

Visualize roots growing from the bottom of your feet, deep into the earth. As they grow down, also picture them growing wide, providing you with a strong, solid foundation. Next, picture energy from the earth coming back up your roots. Imagine the energy as the color red. This energy is nourishing and supporting you. It flows up from your roots; through the soles of your feet; into your legs, pelvic region, abdomen, and chest; out your arms; through your neck and face; and out the top of your head. It is a constant source of flowing energy that reaches all the way up to the sky.

Imagine that you are growing branches from your arms and the top of your head. Your branches extend high, reaching the stars and spreading wide over the horizon. You are a strong, vibrant, magnificent tree, deeply rooted and grounded in the earth while also expansive and connected to the universe. Take a moment to experience your expansiveness. You are enormous.

Now picture energy flowing back down through your branches from the universe. It is radiant white, like sparkling diamonds, and infuses you with love and joy. It flows through your arms, into the crown of your head, and out the bottom of your feet into the earth, penetrating every cell of your body.

Energy is now running in both directions—up to the universe and down to the earth. As it flows through your body, it energizes and cleanses you, freeing you from blockages. Take a moment to experience this flow of pure, dynamic energy. The channels of flowing energy begin to slow down and settle in your heart center, where they mix together and turn a beautiful, radiant pink. Notice as this newly created energy expands from your heart out into the environment. It fills the room you are in, your home, and expands to fill your neighborhood, city, state, and country, until it surrounds the

planet and connects you with all beings. This is your love.
Imagine it circling back to you, surrounding and enveloping
you, penetrating every cell of your being. Bask in this love.

When you feel complete, slowly and gently bring yourself
back to the room and open your eyes. Record your experience
and any new insights that occurred to you. Use this medita-
tion to help you feel grounded, balanced, and connected.

LOOK FOR THE LIGHTHOUSE IN THE STORM

» *Transform Adversity*

> Everything can be taken from a man but one thing: the last of the human freedoms—to choose one's attitude in any given set of circumstances, to choose one's own way.
>
> — Victor Frankl

August 21, 1998. We have just finished our first ocean pas-
sage from Fiji to Vanuatu—four days of utter peace and
beauty, mixed with anxiety and turmoil due to a storm encounter.
I am learning in life that it's not possible to fully appreciate the
peaceful moments without the storms. The storms are what test
and build our character, making us stronger and wiser. In the case
of our passage, the storm added to my sense of adventure and ac-
complishment. True adventure and thus "real living" is found in
the juxtaposition of stormy seas and sunny skies.

Trust in a Higher Purpose

In *Man's Search for Meaning*, a candid and compelling
book about life in the concentration camps of Nazi Ger-
many, Victor Frankl, a survivor, writes that despite an
individual's outward circumstances, he or she has an inner spiritual freedom that cannot be taken away. Because
none of the prisoners knew what the next day might
bring, it was imperative that they have hope for the future. They did not know when the war would end or if
they would be released. The only thing they had control over was their attitude. He states, "It is this spiritual
freedom—which cannot be taken away—that makes life
meaningful and purposeful." With hope and a vision for
the future, people survived. The people who lost hope
died.

Being human, we all experience adversity—pain, suffering, grief. It is part of the human condition. How we

respond is a choice. We can choose to face our trials with courage and a positive attitude, transforming them to create deeper meaning and purpose, or we can remain stuck in our pain and become bitter. Another option is to numb out with addictions such as with food, television, work, alcohol, and drugs. In doing so, we avoid pain but are left feeling dissatisfied, empty, and joyless.

To transform adversity, we need to learn from our trials and allow them to make us stronger, wiser, and more compassionate. In order to learn, it's important to express feelings of pain, anger, grief, and despair so that we can move forward. By expressing gratitude and appreciation for all of the good in our lives and keeping a positive attitude, we are able to come through on the other side of our pain and see the lighthouse in the storm. By giving selflessly to others, our own suffering is transformed.

Transforming adversity means that we choose to take the high road, understanding that there is a greater purpose for our lives and in the challenges we face. We look for the potential lessons and gifts in painful circumstances. Instead of feeling sorry for ourselves and asking, "Why me?" we ask, "How can I learn and grow from this experience?" and "What purpose does this serve in my life and in the lives of those around me?" Sometimes, we are unable to see the higher purpose, but in looking for the lighthouse in the storm, we learn to trust and have faith that there is one.

Express Your Feelings

The storms in our lives build our characters, make us stronger, and cause us to grow in wisdom and love. They teach us about who we are and what we want, lighting our way like moonlight on the ocean at night. But in order to learn and grow from them, we need to be present with our feelings and emotions. We need to experience and express hurt, loss, anger, fear, or despair. If we ignore or deny these feelings, we can remain stuck and ultimately experience more suffering. Further, when we repress our emotions, others can still feel them, which causes them to suffer as well. For example, if you hold in anger, your loved ones may feel like they have to walk on eggshells around you, fearful that you may explode.

When expressing yourself, find constructive, healthy ways to do so, like journaling, talking with a trusted friend or therapist, creating artwork, or playing a musical instrument. When verbalizing your feelings, it is important not to complain and turn it into a "poor me" session. Acknowledge and process your painful experiences, but do not dwell on them. There is a balance between expressing our emotions and getting stuck in them. After you've acknowledged your emotions, attempt to understand the lesson or higher purpose. By seeing the lighthouse in the storm, you will be guided to safer ground, and your difficult emotions will transform.

It may take time, so be patient and don't be afraid to ask for help, which is one of the most courageous things you can do.

If you are currently experiencing a painful situation, such as a dissatisfying job, unhappy marriage, or threatening health condition, take time every day to be present with whatever feelings come up. As you process your emotions, ask yourself, "What can I learn from this experience? Did I have a part in creating the situation?" Maybe you took a job because you needed the income, but it was not what your heart desired. Or maybe you are unhappy with a relationship because you haven't been honest with yourself and the other person. By processing your thoughts, feelings, and emotions, you will gain understanding and clarity and can create action steps to move forward in a positive way.

Sometimes we are unable to do anything to make the situation better. The outward circumstances in our lives at these times are out of our control, such as having a terminal illness. But, as Frankl suggested, we *can* control our attitude and the way we look at things. He wrote, "His unique opportunity lies in the way in which he bears his burden." How do you bear your burdens? Is it with dignity and self-respect? Are you honest with yourself and others about how you feel? Or do you wallow in self-pity? Do you numb your feelings with alcohol, drugs, or other addictions?

As you face your trials with courage and honestly express yourself, not only do you have the opportunity to learn, but you are also an inspiration for others. Like the hero or heroine of a good movie, you can inspire others to reach to the depths of their own reservoir of inner strength and courage.

Transform Through Loss

Watching someone we love suffer and die is one of the most painful experiences we can go through. But as humans, the loss of a loved one is inevitable, so we need to learn to heal and transform our grief in order to live a more purposeful life. Otherwise, grief will weigh us down and keep us from living fully. By transforming grief, we have the opportunity to grow spiritually and expand our experience of love, joy, and compassion. The following story will illustrate this.

Handsome, with blonde hair, blue eyes, and a pale face, he looked like an angel while sleeping. It was May 16, 1999. Sitting in the sterile hospital room of the intensive care unit at my brother's deathbed, I felt nervous while I waited for the perfect opportunity to share important messages with him. Kyle was in and out of sleep but still conscious, and the room, located across from a nurses' station, was noisy. During one of his quiet, wakeful moments, I finally gathered the courage to speak to him.

I talked to him about spirituality and my understanding of what the afterworld was like, hoping to decrease his fear of death. I told him it was okay to *let go* and transition when he was ready. I also said that his twin sister, Kara, would be okay, as they were very close and I didn't want him to worry about her. Tears streamed down his face. As I held his hand, he was able to share his deepest thoughts, fears, and feelings with me—a healing experience for both of us.

Five days later, Kyle died at the age of fifteen from complications with cystic fibrosis, a terminal genetic illness. He was a model of courage as he battled this disease and as he died. His last words were, "It's not so bad." Kyle taught me not to be afraid of death, and as a result, I am free to live without self-imposed limitations.

Three years and three days later, my father died of cancer. (I think he really died of a broken heart, as he loved my brother so much.) He was sixty-four years old and had recently retired after working for the same company for thirty-four years.

Like Kyle, my dad was strong and brave during his battle with cancer. When he surrendered, he died in peace, with his family by his side. His final words were a gift. Not being a religious man, he said, "God, there you are" several times, and his last whispered word was "Kyle." He left us with the knowledge that he was safe and in good hands with his Creator and son.

This experience helped me to further accept death and taught me to go after my dreams *now* and not wait until it's too late.

When we lose someone we love, it's a life-altering experience. With our grief, we are able to tap not only the deepest places of sorrow, fully experiencing our humanity, but also love and joy. Remembering that the depth of our sorrow is in direct proportion to the amount of love we had for the person who has passed on will help with the healing process. Expressing grief is imperative. When stifled, grief weighs us down, causing anger, resentment, and illness. Allowing it to flow like a river will open your heart, creating room for more love, joy, and compassion.

Do you have unexpressed grief due to the death of a loved one? If so, consider creating a meaningful ritual. For example, a year after my brother died, family and friends gathered in a ceremony to plant a tree in his name. On every anniversary, we remember him by hiking to his special tree. Similarly, a year after my father died, we chartered a sailboat and scattered his ashes in a place where he enjoyed sailing. Both of these rituals helped with the transformation of our grief. When choosing a ritual, make it meaningful to you. Also, consider creating a ritual to honor the other losses in your life, such as divorce, changing jobs, or moving away. By acknowledging your losses, you will transform your grief and be able to move forward and experience more love, joy, and purpose in your life.

Be Grateful

In *The Hidden Messages in Water*, Dr. Masaru Emoto demonstrates the power of our thoughts and emotions on water by taking pictures of water crystals after they have been exposed to different words. What he found was that the most beautiful water crystals resulted from the words "love" and "gratitude." Words indicating harm, such as "You fool," did not even form crystals. Since your body is about 70 percent water, your thoughts can have a profound effect on how you feel, so it's important to pay attention to them. With increased awareness, you can work on transforming your thoughts to be more positive, and as a result you will feel better no matter what your life circumstances are.

It can be very difficult to have a positive attitude and feel grateful when we are in the middle of a painful experience. But one of the best ways to transform adversity is to focus our attention on what we love and appreciate rather than on our suffering. For example, after experiencing the death of a loved one, concentrate your thoughts and emotions on what you enjoyed about that person, what their strengths and positive qualities were, and what you learned from them, instead of how much you miss them and long for them to be here again. By focusing on the positive, you do not deny your feelings of sadness, but rather allow them to transform. Try this exercise: after crying and releasing your grief, visualize filling the new space you have created with love and gratitude for the person. Replace your sadness with a positive thought or memory.

By keeping a positive attitude and walking courageously through our trials, not only do we benefit, but we have the opportunity to transform the lives of people around us. Recently, I spent time in Seattle with my seventy-three-year-old father-in-law, Papa, who has Lou Gehrig's disease (ALS), a terminal illness causing muscle degeneration. He is no longer able to do much for himself and spends about sixteen hours a day in bed, using an oxygen machine. When not in bed, he sits in his favorite chair in the family room.

Before visiting, I felt nervous about seeing him, as it had been over six months since our last visit and his condition had worsened. I expected to feel sad and depressed but instead was surprised to feel uplifted. Papa's attitude was so positive, and his faith so strong, my sadness was transformed into joy by being around him. He shared that he doesn't look at ALS as a "terrible thing," but rather as something that "just happened." He doesn't feel sorry for himself, and he is grateful it didn't happen when he was younger. Every day, he makes the best of it and appreciates all he is blessed with. Even though Papa isn't able to do much physically, his loving spirit continues to influence and enrich the lives of those around him. As a result, he is able to experience deep meaning and purpose in his life.

When feeling stuck in the emotions of hopelessness and despair, write in a "gratitude journal." Think about all of the things in your life you are grateful for, such as supportive relationships, loving pets, a comfortable home, work you love, or good health. Also, be specific and focus on some of the small things, like, "I love the color of my office walls" or "I appreciate the yellow daffodils in the front yard." By focusing on what you love and appreciate, your emotions will transform and you will begin to feel better.

Give from Your Heart

When feeling hopeless and depressed, our thoughts are focused primarily on ourselves—on our problems and discomforts. But when we take the focus off of us and put others first, we immediately begin to feel better. Our problems do not seem so insurmountable anymore, because we see we are not alone. Furthermore, when we ease the suffering of others, we also ease our own. There is a spiritual law about the way the universe operates: things come into and out of form and continuously circulate, like our breath. Therefore, that which we give, we receive. For example, if we give love and joy, we will experience love and joy in return.

Giving from the heart is about giving of ourselves—who we are—and being fully present to allow Spirit to flow through us. It doesn't matter how big or small the gift; it is the intention—the love and generosity behind the act—that matters. Seneca, a Roman philosopher and politician, wrote, "The spirit in which a thing is given determines that in which the debt is acknowledged; it's the intention, not the face value of the gift, that's weighed." In other words, it is not *what* we give, but *that* we give and *how* we give. Giving from the heart with joy, and not with reluctance or because of guilt, will benefit you and the receiver.

There are many ways to give. One way is to express gratitude and appreciation to the people in your life on a regular basis by telling them how you feel or giving them a gift, card, or compliment. You can also do something unexpected, like performing your spouse's chores or making their favorite meal. When you give from the heart, do so unconditionally without expecting anything in return; otherwise, it will feel like a sacrifice, and the merit of your generosity will be lost.

If you have gone through a painful experience, consider giving to people now going through what you went through. This will add meaning and purpose to your life while giving others comfort and hope. For example, my family and I volunteer once a year to fund-raise for CFRI (Cystic Fibrosis Research Institute), an organization that does research to find a cure for cystic fibrosis. By giving with our time and energy, we are focusing on something positive rather than wallowing in our grief about Kyle's death. We also feel fulfilled in knowing that because of what we went through, we are making a positive difference in someone else's life.

If you are going through a difficult time and feel depressed, consider reaching out. Is there a meaningful cause you can volunteer for? A neighbor or friend who needs help? What about expressing gratitude to the people in your life?

Try the following exercise: For a week, experiment with giving to whomever you come into contact with. Remember, it can be simple, like giving a smile or compliment or thinking a positive thought about the person. Set your intentions to be present, and ask, "What can I give to this person in this situation?" Maybe they would benefit from your loving presence or kind words. Create a reminder, such as writing on a note card you carry in your pocket or sticky notes you put up in your home, car, and office. Next, allow yourself to gratefully receive the gifts all around you. There is a gift in every moment, so pay attention and receive it!

If you give too much and are feeling depleted, then you are not in balance with the principle of reciprocity. You are giving from an empty vessel rather than a place of overflow. Maybe you have not learned how to receive. It is a circular process: we must be full in order to give, but we can also get filled up by giving. Take time to examine how you give. Is it from an overflow of love, joy, and abundance, or is it causing depletion? If you are depleted, in what ways are you blocking the flow of receiving? In what ways can you allow more abundance into your life? Do you need to work on changing your attitude about giving? Do you need to change *how* you give?

As you give from your heart and are in balance with the flow of reciprocity, your adverse experiences will begin to transform, and your life will have more purpose.

Choose to See the Lighthouse

Our greatest triumphs of humanity—our greatest works of art, poetry, writing, and creation—are often born from adversity. Triumphing over our trials is an inspiration to others, giving hope for all of humanity. Our trials also inspire us to be our best and live up to our fullest potential. But they can do the opposite if we allow them to, causing us to get stuck and be down on life. It's our choice.

A year after Hurricane Katrina hit New Orleans, Lynn, a forty-eight-year-old sales consultant, described the adversity he and his wife experienced and how they were able to move forward without remaining mired in despair.

Having evacuated before the storm and returned home a week later, Lynn described the situation: "There was traffic everywhere. Things were in total chaos." He immediately went into "survival mode" and began patching holes in the roof of his house. Next, Hurricane Rita created an entirely new stress, because he had to leave his home to help family members evacuate in another area. He said, "Here's Rita bearing down on us. It was almost comical." Because of the storm, he spent about a month with his family and was able to bond with his nieces and nephews—a positive experience, despite the stressful situation.

Upon returning, Lynn spent the next five months repairing their house, living in destruction while his wife set up a new home in Colorado. The storm and its aftermath had forced her to move and change jobs. Lynn described their neighborhood as a "ghost town." Curfews were imposed; he had to be back in the city every night by five p.m. There was no gas or electricity at the house; therefore, he had to buy ice for his food and fuel for the generator. Police checkpoints were stationed throughout the city. He had trouble finding food and gas for his car. The smell alone of the three hundred thousand refrigerators thrown out was horrible, not to mention the trash lying around with no one to pick it up.

Despite the destruction all around him, Lynn was able to see the lighthouse in the storm. He said, "I didn't get angry and have a pity party or feel 'poor me.'" Instead, he went with the flow, rolled up his sleeves, and got to work. "When the call is out there, you just have to rise to the occasion and do it," Lynn shared.

Instead of dwelling on the destruction caused to their home, Lynn looked for the positive in the situation. He said, "We were really fortunate. There were people who suffered much more physical loss." Where he lived, he did not experience loss of life. Things could have been much worse. Besides looking for the positive, he also prayed for strength and the resolve to carry on. In addition, he had support from the few remaining people in his neighborhood, who all came together to offer assistance. Lynn shared that "a neighborhood spirit" was created.

Because of Lynn's positive perspective and ability to see the lighthouse in the storm, he was able to move forward with his life. He explained, "I don't take for granted our freedom and rights." He appreciates what he has and realizes what he could have lost.

When we are in the middle of a devastating situation or circumstance in our lives, we may not be able to control what happens around us—like the destruction of Hurricane Katrina—but we do have a choice in how we perceive what is happening and what we do about it. Lynn is a great example of someone who focused on the positive and was empowered to make helpful changes to move forward. He dug deep within himself for the strength and resources he needed to persevere. As a result, when he encounters other storms in his life, he will know he has the courage and faith to navigate through them.

Vicki, a fifty-two-year-old mother of two teenagers, had been diagnosed with stage-four non-Hodgkin's lymphoma, cancer of the cells of the lymphatic system. The diagnosis was sudden and surprising, as she had experienced very few symptoms, had always been a healthy person, and did not have a history of cancer in her family.

"I always thought, 'I am going through this for a reason,'" explained Vicki. She never felt sorry for herself or asked, "Why me?" Instead, she asked, "What can I learn from this experience?"

Moreover, she wanted to be a positive example for her family and friends, especially her children. She had many role models who had prepared her in advance. By watching others triumph over their trials, she learned she had a choice: to accept what was happening and make the best of it or to wallow in negativity.

Vicki believes in the Buddhist philosophy that says, "Pain and suffering is a result of resisting what is." She said, "When we resist and are in a state of fear, anger, and resentment, we create energy that doesn't heal."

Vicki's positive attitude and ability to accept what is has been a process. She continually works to keep herself from slipping into negativity and old behavior patterns by journaling, doing daily meditations and guided imagery, and reading books. Plus, the support of family and friends has given her the strength to carry on. "The support I got from everyone was just awesome. It was eye-opening," she recalls. A friend organized rides to her chemotherapy sessions and food for the family. Her refrigerator and freezer had "never looked so full and will never look that full again."

As a result of this trial in her life, Vicki shared, "I have more gratitude for so many things I took for granted." Her friendships have become closer and stronger. Furthermore, she wants to give back by being of service and helping others. She wants to be able to say, "I've made this world a better place."

The cancer is now in remission and is expected to remain so for another ten years or more. Vicki's positive attitude, faith in a higher power, and commitment to healing have helped her through adversity and transformed her. It may have even saved her life.

Every moment of every day we have the power to choose how we look at what shows up in our lives. We can resist our difficult experiences, causing more pain and suffering, or we can transform them by looking for the lighthouse in the storm and having faith that there is a greater purpose. If we dwell in the emotions of despair and remain struck in grief, we will not allow the miracle of hope, rebirth, and new life to emerge. If we step on a budding flower, blocking it from the sun, it is unable to grow and blossom. By allowing ourselves to reach for the sun, see the light, and grow and blossom from the tragedies and trials we face, we are able to make meaning out of them and do something positive with our lives.

Allow your trials to strengthen you. Allow them to motivate you to reach within the depths of your being and become the person you are meant to be.

Exercises

1. Describe your own personal stories about how you have been victimized ("poor me," "why me?"). Focus on the places where you hold anger, resentment, and grief. On a scale from 1 to 10 (1 = not at all, 10 = very much), how much do these stories affect your life today? What can you do to decrease that number by at least one point? Explain.

2. If you are currently experiencing adversity in your life, are you being honest with yourself and others about how you feel? Or are you repressing your emotions? Take time to process your painful experiences through journaling, talking to a trusted friend or

therapist, or expressing yourself creatively through music or art.

3. Have you experienced the death of a loved one or other major losses in your life? Where are you with the grieving process? Are you holding back tears of sadness? If so, allow yourself time and space to grieve. Tune in to your body to see where the grief may be stuck, and visualize sending light and love to this area. Create a meaningful ritual to assist with the transformation process.

4. One of the best ways to keep a positive attitude is by expressing gratitude on a daily basis. Create a list of all the things you are grateful for and post it somewhere you can easily see it. Start a "gratitude journal" and write in it when feeling sorry for yourself. Begin each day with a gratitude prayer or meditation, and look for the gifts that are all around you.

5. Take time to examine how you give. Is it from an overflow of love, joy, and abundance, or is it making you feel depleted? Are you blocking the flow of receiving? In what ways can you allow more abundance into your life to create balance and reciprocity? Notice how you feel when giving unconditionally from your heart. Do you receive back what you give? Explain.

Guided Meditation

The purpose of this meditation is to experience a feeling of gratitude for all that you are and all that is in your life.

Sit comfortably in a chair or cross-legged on a cushion on the floor with your back upright and your hands resting on your lap. Begin by bringing your focus of awareness inside to the core of your being. Notice your breath and allow it to deepen with each inhalation. Create a rhythmic flow by equally spacing your in-breath and out-breath. As you begin to relax, notice any areas in your body that feel tense or uncomfortable, and send breath to them, allowing the tension to soften and release. Next, notice the quality of your thoughts. Attempt to still your mind as you sit peacefully in silent awareness.

Go within your body and begin to pay attention to all of the functions it is performing to keep you alive without your effort. Start with your head. Your brain is working twenty-four hours a day, your eyes take in the beauty around you, your mouth and nose breathe in oxygen, your ears hear the sounds of creation, and even your eyelashes perform a function by protecting your eyes. Continue down your throat, into your chest. Feel the pulsing beat of your heart. It is pumping blood throughout your entire being. Pay attention to the inside of your belly. Your stomach, intestines, and colon are working together to bring nutrients to your blood. Your entire body is an incredible organism of millions of parts working together automatically. Not only are you a miraculous physical creation, but a spiritual wonder as well. You have a unique personality and special talents and gifts, different from anyone else in the entire world. Take a moment to imagine all of your good qualities. With each breath, relax deeper into a state of love and gratitude for the miracle that you are.

Visualize everything that you love and appreciate in your life: the people who love and support you, your home, your pets, your work, and the natural beauty of the earth—the trees, flowers, birds, and animals. As each image crosses your mind, surround it with love and appreciation. Picture light flowing from your heart and hugging the person or image you are grateful for. Spend some time here and bask in the wonderful feeling of giving gratitude from your heart and receiving the gift of love back. Feel the warmth and love of your connection to life itself. You are grateful to be alive!

When you feel complete, slowly and gently bring yourself back to the room and open your eyes. Record your experience and any new insights that occurred to you. Try this meditation when feeling depressed or sorry for yourself.

STEP 8

SAIL DOWNWIND, SURFING THE WAVES

» *Trust and Let Go*

Happiness cannot be found through great
effort and willpower, but is already there,
in relaxation and letting go. Nothing to
do, nothing to force, nothing to want, and
everything happens by itself.

—LAMA GENDUN RINPOCHE

September 10, 1998. Stepping out of the companionway into the cockpit for my 8:30 a.m. watch, I am relieved to see sunny blue skies. The squalls have finally passed. Beyond the stern of the boat appear large, twelve-foot waves, a result of the stormy weather. Sailing downwind, surfing the waves, my stomach drops, similar to the sensation when riding a roller coaster. It's exhilarating and fun. Surrendering to the ocean's power, I feel relaxed and at peace.

Sail Downwind with the Waves

While sailing in the South Pacific and encountering storms, our boat was headed downwind with the waves, and as a result, we were more comfortable and at ease. Had we been heading against the wind and waves, we would have suffered greatly. This is a metaphor for our lives and speaks to the importance of going with the flow, accepting what is, and trusting we will be taken care of. When we resist life, like going against the wind and waves, we cause suffering for ourselves and others.

Resistance is the result of fear, which causes constriction—tension and anxiety. This robs us of experiencing joy and keeps us from moving forward. Since we live in a culture that capitalizes on fear, it's difficult to trust and let go. The media constantly reminds us of the need to protect ourselves from natural disasters, diseases, and crime, causing us to live in a state of anxiety. As a result, we strangle life by holding on too tightly in an attempt to control it, and in the process, we often create the very thing we fear. For example, a pregnant friend recently shared her experience of watching a television program about women in childbirth and the complications that can arise. The show scared her and caused her to be anxious about her upcoming labor. As a result, it may be difficult for her to relax during the process.

The only truth we know is that nothing is permanent. The very nature of life is change. Everything that comes into form eventually changes form. Everything that is given birth to eventually dies. Everything that is created eventually ceases to exist. Therefore, our attempts to hold on go against the very fabric of life—of the one truth we know to be fact—and result in suffering. For example, even death creates a change of form and the possibility for something new, but we spend so much of our time, energy, and money trying to avoid it. By running and hiding from the one thing that is inevitable, we resist life, which causes us to feel stressed and unfulfilled.

Trust, on the other hand, induces a feeling of openness, lightness, and freedom. It requires that we accept what is in our lives, surrender to the outcome, and let go of our attachments. By trusting the ever-changing nature of life, we can relax and go with the flow, like sailing downwind and surfing the waves. When experiencing more play, laughter, and fun in our lives, we are receptive to allowing our highest good and can sail smoothly into the life of our dreams.

Trusting and letting go is like sailing in the "groove" instead of being stuck in the "no-go zone"—an area in which a boat going into the wind cannot produce the power to sail. When sailing in the groove, the sails are trimmed to perfection, allowing for maximum speed given the wind conditions. Heading on a comfortable course, all feels right with the world.

Surrender to the Outcome

To surrender means to fully relax into the present moment with acceptance and love—to relinquish control to a higher power (God/Creator), knowing there is a plan for our lives and that we are being fully supported to fulfill our purpose. Surrendering is not about giving up and becoming hopeless, but about giving *it* up—our ideas and beliefs about the way life should be—to a higher intelligence that has our highest good in mind.

As we surrender, it's not necessary to give up our dreams and desires, as they fuel our passion. But we need to let go of our expectations of what they will look like and how and when they will show up—the outcome. When we have expectations, we set ourselves up for disappointment. By being patient and trusting that there is a higher purpose and plan for our lives that is unfolding in divine perfection, we are better able to live in the moment and show up every day with all of our energy present and available.

It's a delicate balancing act to allow our desires to propel us into action while at the same time letting go of our attachment to the outcome. For example, if you are having difficulty getting pregnant, instead of giving up, you take action by having tests done to ensure things are working properly, and by showing up at the most opportune time every month to make love with your partner, but you let go of your attachment to the results. In the process, you have not given up your desire, but you have surrendered to the outcome, trusting the higher purpose for your life. As a result, you are able to show up in a much more relaxed state of mind and can enjoy the experience.

The following are signs indicating that you may be in a place of fear, instead of trust, and are trying to control the outcome: needing for everything and everyone, including ourselves, to be perfect; trying to control someone else's behavior; wanting things our way; being inflexible, rigid, and unwilling to change; thinking of ourselves as right and everyone else as wrong; and being overly responsible, believing we are the only ones who can get the job done.

For example, when I received the call that my father was hospitalized with cancer, I immediately succumbed to fear and tried to control the outcome by praying for him to live, buying guided meditations for him to listen to, and trying to find healthy foods he could eat. I wanted him to heal and for things to go *my way*.

The process of surrendering and letting go was like an emotional roller coaster of hope, despair, hope, despair, and, finally, acceptance. For instance, my father almost died during the first week of being hospitalized, due to an infection caused by chemotherapy. The doctors suggested letting him go, but my family and I were too upset and opted to put him on life support. Miraculously, he recovered from the infection and was taken off life support, defying the doctor's predictions and therefore causing us to have hope in further healing. Other miracles of healing occurred as well—not physically, as we desired, but emotionally and spiritually. One was the time my stepmom read their wedding vows to him while he was on life support. He appeared to be unconscious, but cried.

Finally, before his death, I was able to accept his condition and surrender. As a result, I could relax, be more present and available, and experience the sacredness of the moment when he took his final breath.

Are there circumstances in your life you are having difficulty accepting, but that are out of your control? If so, ask to be shown how to surrender and let go. Say the following twelve-step prayer: "God grant me the serenity to accept the things I cannot change, the courage to change the things I can, and the wisdom to know the difference." Pray to be shown what you do have control over and what actions to take. Then relax and let go.

By surrendering our lives, we are able to show up every day open and available, with all of our energy present, to experience a life of passion and purpose.

Let Go of Your Attachments

Learning to trust is an ongoing, lifetime process. An important step in that process is to let go of our attachments. When we are too attached to a dream, belief, idea, relationship, or material object, we create stagnant energy that binds and limits us, often depleting the very energy we need to create what we truly desire. Letting go of our attachments may involve a grieving process, but as we grieve, surrender, and let go, we create room for something new to appear—many times the very thing we wanted in the first place. The story below is an illustration.

In the fenced-in meadow behind our house in Big Bear lived two horses and three burros. Over the past two years, I had developed a strong appreciation for these animals and frequently enjoyed watching them graze. One day, they disappeared when the property was sold and they were moved. I felt sad and grieved. The very next day, twenty-one wild, healthy burros showed up to graze and play in the open meadow. They were a pleasure to listen to and watch.

Grieving and letting go of my attachment to the original horses and burros created room for me to experience joy when the wild ones showed up.

Maybe you have completed a project but are still holding on to it, therefore tying up the energy that would allow you to continue creating. When we create from our essence, from our passion, it feels like giving birth to new life. Whether it's a painting, a book, music, or starting a new business, we can become attached to our creations, which gets us stuck and keeps us from moving forward. For instance, a friend was recently advised to perform a ceremony to symbolically let go of all of the writing projects she had created over the years. As she conducted the ceremony, she was surprised to experience grief. She had been holding these projects near to her heart. But once she acknowledged her grief and consciously engaged in the act of letting go, she had more room and freedom to express her passion and create anew.

One of the most difficult areas in which we need to let go of our attachments is our relationships. This does not mean we necessarily need to let go of the relationship, but rather our *attachment* to it—trying to control the other person, or needing them to fulfill us and make us happy. When we let go, we are giving the relationship room to breathe and can therefore experience more enjoyment. We also need to let go of our attachments to the roles we play, such as mother, father, husband, wife, sister, brother, friend, colleague, or business entrepreneur. Letting go of our attachments to our roles frees us to be who we truly are: magnificent, limitless spiritual beings.

Take a moment to review your life. Where are you holding on too tightly? What are you afraid of losing? If you feel disappointed that things did not work out the way you thought they should, or you fear losing something, such as a relationship or the outcome of a dream, you are probably too attached. Strong emotions such as fear or despair may be a sign that you are holding on too tightly and trying to control the outcome.

Try the following exercise: Write your attachments individually on separate strips of paper and crinkle them up. Remember to include the roles you play, such as mother, father, partner, or friend. Meditate on where you feel the attachment residing in your body. For example, do you feel tension in your stomach or head when you think of it? Next, blow the energy of each attachment into your strips of paper. Toss them into a fire one at a time, focusing your intention on letting go. Notice how you feel as the energy of your attachments is released into the fire.

If you are attached to a dream, belief, idea, role, relationship, or material object, ask, "What does it represent? What need does it fulfill?" For instance, the desire to conceive a baby might be about experiencing uncon-ditional love and joy. Are there other ways to have this need met, like buying a pet or adopting a child? Some-times what we think we want may not be what we truly desire. Search deep within yourself for your truth.

Like carrying a backpack filled with rocks, our attach-ments create a heavy burden. When we trust and let them go, we take off that backpack and feel lighter and freer.

Relax and Go with the Flow

As we accept what is, surrender to the outcome, and let go of our attachments, we allow the energy of resistance to melt away and are able to relax and go with the flow. When in the flow, we don't attempt to force things to happen or resist things that are happening. Instead of trying, pushing, or fighting, we allow things to unfold naturally, in divine perfection. Everything is done with ease, like sailing downwind and surfing the waves.

By either forcing a particular outcome or resisting what is, we step out of the co-creator role and into "*my will be done.*" It's like saying to God, or a higher power, "I don't trust you to take care of me and provide for my highest good." Since we don't always know what is in our highest good, our efforts of force or resistance are futile.

Allowing, on the other hand, creates a feeling of openness, lightness, and freedom. When in this state, we are better able to be in the moment, remaining present with our body, mind, and soul. This allows Spirit to work through us, and everything in our life flows smoothly and naturally.

My writing process is a good example. After setting my intentions for what I want to create, I let go of my expectations of how or when it will happen and show up present and available to Spirit's guidance. The minute I try to make it happen, I feel stuck and get frustrated. My writing doesn't flow. So instead, I express my intentions, relax, and let go of the outcome. Often, I don't have a clue about how it will unfold. Something will come to me early in the morning, during a dream, while meditating, or spontaneously while I am journaling—but rarely when I hold expectations about how it should go. For example, lying in bed the other day, I debated whether or not to go to church or stay home and work on this book. As my deadline was soon approaching, it made logical sense to stay home and continue writing. But my inner wisdom guided me to get up and go to church. Sure enough, the sermon was on the exact topic I was writing about and gave me the additional information I needed to move forward. Co-creating this way requires little effort on my part and is very enjoyable. All I have to do is show up, set my intentions, and listen for Spirit's guidance.

Nature is a wonderful teacher of this principle of flow. We have only to look at the seasons of spring, summer, fall, and winter and the cycles of life and death. Just like nature, we have our own natural cycles. For instance, there is a time for healing, a time for going backward to release what we have stored up along the way in terms of sadness, anger, and disappointment. During this time, we must allow ourselves the space to let go so that when the season changes, we will have room to experience more love, joy, and abundance.

We need to be loving and patient with ourselves during these uncomfortable periods and trust that the season will change when the time is right. If we are too hard on ourselves, resisting the season we are in, we will suffer and block the natural flow of healing and abundance. For example, if you are sick, instead of resisting it by pretending you feel good or trying to make yourself feel better, surrender. Accept your situation, relax, and allow for healing to take place naturally. The more you resist being ill, the worse you will feel.

If you are frequently thinking about how you are going to improve yourself or your circumstances so *it*— your dream, perfect health, a relationship, or job—can happen, you may be resisting and trying to control the outcome. Instead, work on creating a positive vision of what you want. Trust your highest good is on its way to you right now. Relax and let go.

As you relax, creative ideas will flow rapidly, and you will get more accomplished with less effort. Staying in an open and positive place, you are more receptive to allowing your highest good.

Play, Laugh, and Have Fun

One of the best ways to relax and open ourselves up to the flow is through play. As adults, we've been taught about the value of hard work and being responsible, but in the process, we have lost our ability to be spontaneous and play. Most of us are in a constant state of tension and take life too seriously, going from our responsibilities at work to our responsibilities at home. Play helps us relax and balances stress and hard work, bringing more joy into our lives.

Playing requires that we follow our hearts and do what we love and feel passionate about while leaving our worries behind and being fully present in the moment. Babies and small children find joy in the simple things. Everything is new and exciting; even banging pots and pans can give them immeasurable pleasure. They have no worries about the future and are totally present in the moment. Kittens, puppies, and dolphins are also great teachers of play, being spontaneous and rambunctious. What would your inner child enjoy doing? Teasing, joking with friends, playing sports or games, being silly, playing with children or pets, dancing, singing? When was the last time you had fun? What were you doing? The following story is an example of how play can turn a potentially boring situation into fun.

While anchored off Thursday Island, a very small and sleepy town located on the northeastern tip of Australia, John and I were bored while waiting for our laundry to be done. Feeling unfulfilled hanging out at the local pub, we decided to explore, and we happened on a park. As John slumbered under a tree, I decided to join the kids on the playground. *Why not? I will never be too old to play,* I told myself. While swinging, I attempted to start a conversation with the young girl next to me. After getting no response, I synchronized my swinging with hers and looked backward and upside-down, making funny faces at her, as the swing lifted me high in the air. Finally, her walls broke down and she began giggling. After swinging, she took my hand and showed me around the rest of the playground. We played on every piece of equipment, including the monkey bars. We even climbed a tree. Boredom quickly disappeared, and I felt joyful, young, and alive.

Reflecting on that day, I learned how easy it is to turn a boring and meaningless experience into a fulfilling one by making the most of my surroundings and reaching out. I also realized that sometimes it is the small things we do every day that can be tedious that can also be fun. It's our choice.

As we choose to play more, we need to remember to laugh. Laughter is the best medicine for the soul. It opens our heart, releases tension, and makes us more receptive, creating space for the flow of abundance, creativity, love, and joy. What makes you laugh? Try putting comics, jokes, and funny pictures around your house or office. Rent funny movies. Laugh at your imperfections. Find humor in life.

We need to loosen up and lighten up, stop taking life so seriously, and find ways to bring more laughter, play, and silliness into our lives on a daily basis. Dare to break free from your inner restrictions. Do something outrageous, play like a kid, and have fun!

Commit to Follow Your Heart

When living an authentic life and following our dreams, it can feel like we're out at the end of a tree limb or at the edge of a cliff. It's not always comfortable. We may not know where the next month's mortgage payment or rent check is coming from, or how the bills are going to be paid. It's easier to trust when our bank account is full. But the universe has an incredible way of assisting us when we are committed to living our dreams. Resources show up unexpectedly to help with our plans, like money, people, or books with important information. Signs appear and synchronistic events occur.

For example, before leaving Seattle, John and I received unexpected money on several occasions, which greatly helped with our plans. Similarly, after moving to Big Bear and starting my own business, resources and support showed up that I could never have dreamed of. As we forged ahead despite our financial uncertainties, we continued to be provided for again and again. The following quote by W. H. Murray has been an inspiration to us along the way:

> Until one is committed, there is hesitancy, the chance to draw back, always ineffectiveness. Concerning all acts of initiative (and creation), there is one elementary truth the ignorance of which kills countless ideas and splendid plans: that the moment one definitely commits oneself, then providence moves too.
>
> A whole stream of events issues from the decision, raising in one's favor all manner of unforeseen incidents, meetings and material assistance, which no man could have dreamt would have come his way.

Commitment is essential when endeavoring to live our dreams. If we commit only halfway, we are giving the universe mixed signals, and we close the door to receiving assistance. Once we fully commit, the doors fly open and assistance comes pouring in from all directions. The level of success we achieve—in any endeavor—directly correlates to our level of commitment. Our job is to decide what it is we truly desire, commit with all of our hearts, and trust and let go while the universe works its magic.

Sandy, a screenwriter, had a consulting business for thirteen years. When she was no longer enjoying her business, she decided to sell it and move. This gave her an opportunity to follow her passion for writing and also lead trips to the Galapagos Islands.

As a business owner, she had learned to trust that she would be provided for, since the business had its ups and downs. She said, "I knew something would happen to take care of me, because it always did."

Sandy decided to sell her house in Long Beach, California, and move into her home in Big Bear because she did not want to go back to work at a regular job. She shared, "I didn't want to sell myself out by working just to pay the mortgage."

When she first moved to Big Bear, Sandy was not sure how she would make a living, but she trusted the money would come by doing what she loved. She made a commitment to follow her heart. She began doing environmental work because it was important to her, and sure enough, several months later, she unexpectedly started getting paid for it.

When asked how she learned to trust, Sandy said, "It's a lifetime process. Even when you learn to trust at one level, something else comes up and you have to reinstitute trust all over again."

Sandy has worked hard to retrain her mind from thinking negative, fearful thoughts. In the past, she used a technique called *thought stopping* to redirect her thinking. "You become an observer of what is going on inside of you. You take control and don't have to listen to where your mind wants to go," Sandy explained.

Retraining your mind to be in the moment and think positive thoughts takes vigilance and practice, but it is well worth the effort. Today, Sandy frequently finds she is without thoughts and feels more at peace. She joked, "Sometimes being out of your mind is a good thing!"

Cathy, an interior designer, started her own business a couple of years ago after moving to San Diego. Being divorced and not knowing anyone in the area was challenging. She shared, "I don't have anyone else to depend on to lighten the load." What helps Cathy keep her faith and remain positive is to walk on the beach for about an hour every other day. She said, "Being outside, breathing the fresh air, and being in nature clears my mind and helps me to feel grateful."

When out of work for months at a time, Cathy felt scared but "kept following the pull and went with it." As a result of listening to her intuition and letting her feelings and emotions guide her, she is now experiencing success. During the process, she continued to trust that she would be taken care of, and she remained committed to her vision. Her level of trust and commitment is in proportion to the level of success she is experiencing today.

With experience and learning from family and friends, Cathy has come to accept life and is in a peaceful place. She shared, "I believe more and more, the older I get, that things will be the way they are meant to be."

By making a commitment to following our hearts and trusting the process, doors open as providence moves in to assist us. All forces come together as in a beautiful symphony of love, joy, and abundance. When we surf the waves, sailing smoothly into the life of our dreams, our hearts are satisfied and fulfilled.

Exercises

1. Are there circumstances in your life that you are having difficulty accepting but that are out of your control? If so, explain. How might you surrender more deeply? Write the following twelve-step prayer on a note card and place it where you can see it: "God grant me the serenity to accept the things I cannot change, the courage to change the things I can, and the wisdom to know the difference."

2. To what are you holding on too tightly—an idea, belief, relationship, or dream? What are you afraid of losing by letting go? Journal and explain. Create a fire ceremony to burn the energy of your attachments. Then do a meditation to visualize feeling lighter and freer.

3. What are you trying to force to make happen? What are you resisting? Say the following affirmation to yourself on a daily basis, until you feel more open, relaxed, and receptive: "I allow the natural unfolding of my deepest desires in divine perfection, for the highest good. I trust that God's/Creator's plan for me is even better than I can imagine."

4. Are you creating room in your life for play? Are you enjoying yourself and having fun? If not, sit quietly in meditation and ask your inner child what it would like to experience. Then set aside part of your schedule to create more time for these experiences. Make a commitment to bringing more joy, laughter, and fun into your life every day.

5. Have you committed yourself fully to following your heart and living the life of your dreams? If not, what are you afraid of? During meditation, ask your higher self to show you a vision of what your life might look like if you were to fully commit to your dreams. Journal about your experience and then

create an action plan of the steps you can take to demonstrate your commitment.

Guided Meditation

This meditation will help you to relax deeply within yourself and experience the freedom and peace that comes from completely surrendering and letting go.

If possible, sit directly in the sunlight either in a chair, cross-legged on a cushion, or outdoors in nature. Begin by focusing on your breath, allowing it to deepen with each inhalation. Create a rhythmic flow by equally spacing your in-breath and out-breath. As you begin to relax, notice any areas in your body that feel tense or uncomfortable, and send breath to them, allowing the tension to soften and release. Notice the quality of your thoughts. Attempt to still your mind as you sit peacefully in silent awareness.

Imagine a warm, golden ball of light about the size of a basketball floating a few feet above your head. It slowly sinks down, entering your crown, and fills all of the space within your head, melting away any tension, negative thoughts, and worries. Sinking down farther, it travels through your neck, into your chest, arms, and hands, and out your fingertips. Imagine it flowing through your abdomen and pelvic region, down through your thighs and calves, and out through your feet into the earth. As this amazing golden light travels through your body, it penetrates every cell of your being, filling you with light, love, and peace. It dissolves areas where you are holding on too tightly, helping you to relax deeply, surrender, and let go. Feel the warmth of its energy, like you are basking in the sun. You are completely free and at peace within yourself.

Picture the light flowing out from your body a few feet from your skin, encompassing your energy body. Visualize it radiating from you, filling and surrounding your home. It travels even farther to encompass your neighborhood, community, and state. Picture it surrounding your nation and, even farther, the entire planet. See the planet filled with and surrounded by this incredible brilliant light. Notice it continuing to spread even farther out into space, filling the dark emptiness, surrounding the stars and planets, flowing throughout the galaxy and entire universe. Bask in the peace and warmth of this expanded state. You are a loving, light-filled being connected to all that is. You are one with the universe and all of life.

When you feel complete, slowly and gently bring yourself back to the room and open your eyes. Record your experience and any new insights that occurred to you. Try this meditation when feeling tense or stressed.

PART V

ARRIVE
AT YOUR
DESTINATION

RE-CREATE YOUR LIFE FROM JOY

> We must learn to reawaken and keep our-
> selves awake, not by mechanical aids, but by
> an infinite expectation of the dawn, which
> does not forsake us even in our soundest
> sleep.
>
> —HENRY DAVID THOREAU

Experiencing joy is what the journey is about; therefore,
arriving at our destination is elusive, because as creative,
infinite beings, we are always reinventing ourselves and
re-evaluating who we are and what we desire. When
we fulfill one desire, another is born, and then another.
It's a never-ending process; we will forever be creating
anew. Therefore, it's all about the *journey* and living our
desires on a daily basis. When we are too focused on the
destination, whether it's our to-do list, goals, or dreams,
we miss out on experiencing joy now and may miss an
island paradise just off of our plotted course.

In the movie *Before Sunset*, Ethan Hawke's character says, "Happiness is in the doing. Not in getting what you want." Happiness can only be found in the process and in the moment. Therefore, the dream is right here, right now, not on some distant shore.

How we see and experience our world—the internal state of our being—determines our consciousness. It is this state of consciousness that we bring into our life experiences that matters. As Eckhart Tolle writes in *A New Earth*, "Joy does not come from what you do, it flows into what you do and thus into this world from deep within you." It doesn't matter what we do or accomplish. If we are fully awake and conscious, we will feel a heightened sense of purpose in whatever we do and will experience joy. For example, say you're doing the dishes. If you're unconscious—thinking about work, your to-do list, what you're going to make for dinner—you are going through the motions, and your actions are only about getting the job done. Therefore, you will experience no sense of fulfillment. But, if you are fully conscious, present, and awake, you can enjoy even the most mundane tasks.

The awakening and transformation process is about the inward journey we take while heading toward the destination of our dreams. Awakening, evolving, and growing takes time, but like a sailboat tacking through the ocean, steady progress is assuredly made when we set out to re-create our selves and our lives. The following story about Laura, a sixty-year-old artist, illustrates this point.

Early on, Laura knew she was a painter but was discouraged by her family from pursuing her passion. "Artists are supposed to be poor" was a limiting belief passed on to her, so she received a teaching credential instead. When she was forty-five, several major life-changing incidents occurred: her mother had a stroke, her stepmother was diagnosed with cancer, and her first husband died. She realized, "I could die at any time," and decided to quit her job to pursue painting. Thus began her journey, a twelve-year process of finding work she loves while enjoying life.

For ten years, she did commission work that didn't flow from her heart. She said, "It was killing me. I felt very little enthusiasm. It was a scramble to make money, and I was frequently sick." Feeling up against a wall because she couldn't afford to quit her business but desperately needed a time-out, Laura went to speak with people at her church. Room and board at a mountain camp were offered in exchange for help remodeling cabins. Laura gladly accepted.

Preparing to leave, she gave things away, sold stuff, and put money into savings. "Walking away from my business was like jumping into the unknown. It was scary, but I closed my eyes and did it," Laura said. When leaving, she thought she would be coming back in about six months. Four years later, she's still living at the camp.

Initially, she had no cell phone, television, computer, or phone, and she communicated with friends and family through letters. "I needed the space to clear my head, and the next thing just presented its self," she shared. Living a stress-free life without time constraints, Laura's artwork was able to emerge.

It has been a process. She explained, "It took time for me to realize I have this unique gift and purpose, and this is what I'm supposed to do. I had to come to know I deserved to be doing what I was doing." Through therapy, she was able to transform her fears and limiting beliefs as well as release emotional baggage from the past. As a result, space was created for her painting to flow and be prolific.

Laura shared, "It comes through me. When I'm painting, I'm really not there. That's part of how I know this is my job. I'm in the flow—it's easy and comfortable." She is having fun doing what she loves and is experiencing joy in the process. She added, "I'm very at ease and at peace."

Where are you on your inward journey of transformation? Do you feel at ease and at peace? Are you experiencing joy in the moment? Are you consciously making choices that are in alignment with who you are and your deepest dreams and desires?

The time is now to set sail and re-create your life from a place of joy. As you make a commitment to living your best life today, you will sail into the life of your dreams—a purposeful, joyful experience in this moment of now.

TIME TO PLOT
A NEW COURSE

I left the woods for as good a reason as why
I went there. Perhaps it seemed to me that I
had several more lives to live, and could not
spare any more time for that one.

—Henry David Thoreau

During the writing of this book, several seasons have passed and our lives and dreams have changed. The biggest decision we made was to sell the sailboat and cabin and move to Colorado. The vision for our move was to experience more opportunity and prosperity. We wanted to create room in our lives for personal and financial growth—and to start a family. In Colorado, we could maintain our lifestyle of living in nature at a slower pace, while being only thirty minutes from a large metropolitan city with more opportunities.

During the process of moving and letting go, I experienced a lot of grief, as I loved the home we had created, the community where we lived, and the friends I had made. Many times, I questioned whether we were making the right decision. Further, stepping into the unknown was scary. But every time I sat silently in meditation, I experienced a feeling of joy and lightness. My higher self knew the move was in our highest good. Plus, synchronistic events continued to unfold to show us that yes, this was the way to go. John flew to Denver for a job interview and to rent a house. He had been looking at properties in the city that we could get by with until buying our own home in the mountains. At the very last minute, he checked the newspaper one more time for mountain properties about thirty minutes from Denver. Sure enough, a new listing had appeared—the perfect cabin and home for us, completely surrounded by nature.

As I processed my feelings and grief about the move, I decided to focus on the idea that I was expanding my life rather than losing something. I saw how all of my experiences living in Big Bear and owning a sailboat were forever etched in my heart and a part of who I am. I realized that by moving and re-creating our lives, we were only adding to our experiences and enhancing ourselves. My grief was quickly transformed as I held this new consciousness of expansion versus loss. I also trusted life to provide us with "this or even better." I knew that once we committed to this new direction, providence would move in to help—as it always had.

Shortly after settling into our new home, I knew we had made the right decision. While driving into town, I see elk and horses grazing, snowcapped mountains set against a pristine blue sky appearing in the distance, and aspen trees dotting the hills with yellow, gold, orange, and red. New friends are rapidly appearing, and opportunities are opening up for both of us. I'm in awe of the divine perfection and flow of our lives as this magical journey continues to unfold.

Karen Mehringer
Evergreen, Colorado
September 2006

ACKNOWLEDGMENTS

Creator, I am so grateful for the honor of co-creating this book and bringing it into the world. It's been an amazing journey of personal transformation, healing, fun, and joy. Thank you. Thank you. Thank you.

Sail into Your Dreams was created from a collaboration of ideas, inspiration, energy, and effort. Thank you to Denise Zuckerman for planting the seed to go for it. Many thanks also to Diana Guerrero for guiding me in the right direction with the concept and for suggesting helpful resources. To my readers—Sandy Steers (who is also my writing and creative partner), Denise Cavali, Christie Walker, Cathleen Calkins, Laura Jaster, and my dear husband, John Mehringer—I am forever grateful for your support and valuable feedback.

I also want to acknowledge my spiritual mentors, teachers, and friends—John Knowlton, Lumenaria Goyer, Robin Bradley, and Lena Karunemaya. Your wisdom and love is infused within these pages. My meditation group has also been a source of support, inspiration, and spiritual growth. Thank you to Robin, Gina, Carol, Sandy, and Sue for being there for me.

To all of my clients and workshop participants from whom I learn so much, and to all of the people interviewed for this book—thank you. Your lives and stories are an inspiration.

To Carrie Obry, my editor at Llewellyn—I am grateful for your belief in me and this project. Thank you for your warmth, receptivity, and enthusiasm. You have been a joy to work with. And to the rest of the staff at Llewellyn—Wade, Alison, Kelly, et al—thanks for your hard work and dedication. Thanks also to Barbara Neighbors Deal, with Literary Associates, for believing in this book and supporting me on my journey to publication.

Mom, I am so grateful for your love and support. You are my biggest fan and have always encouraged me to do anything I want in life. You are an amazing role model of someone who lives a purposeful life, who is not afraid to go after your dreams.

I am incredibly blessed to have such supportive family on both sides, including my in-laws. Thank you for your love. You have all enriched my life.

Last, but not least, I want to acknowledge my husband, John, whose love and support has made the creation of this book possible. Honey, you are a joy to be with on this journey! I love you!

RECOMMENDED READING

Here is a list of books that have been helpful on my journey.

Deepak Chopra, *The Seven Spiritual Laws of Success: A Practical Guide to the Fulfillment of Your Dreams* (Navato, CA: New World Library, 1994)

Deepak Chopra, *The Spontaneous Fulfillment of Desire: Harnessing the Infinite Power of Coincidence* (New York: Crown Publishing Group, 2003)

Dr. Wayne W. Dyer, *10 Secrets of Success and Inner Peace* (Carlsbad, CA: Hay House, Inc., 2001)

Dr. Wayne W. Dyer, *The Power of Intention: Learning to Co-create Your World Your Way* (Carlsbad, CA: Hay House, Inc., 2004)

Dr. Wayne W. Dyer, *There's a Spiritual Solution to Every Problem* (New York: HarperCollins, 2001)

Masaru Emoto, *The Hidden Messages in Water* (Hillsboro, OR: Beyond Words Publishing, 2004)

Debbie Ford, *The Best Year of Your Life: Dream It. Plan It. Live It* (San Francisco, CA: HarperSanFrancisco, 2005)

Shakti Gawain, *Creative Visualization: Use the Power of Your Imagination to Create What You Want in Your Life* (Navato, CA: New World Library, 1995)

Louise L. Hay, *You Can Heal Your Life* (Carlsbad, CA: Hay House, Inc., 1999)

Esther and Jerry Hicks, *Ask and It Is Given: Learning to Manifest Your Desires* (Carlsbad, CA: Hay House, Inc., 2004)

Catherine Ingram, *Passionate Presence: Experiencing the Seven Qualities of Awakened Awareness* (New York: Penguin Putnam, 2003)

Henriette Klauser, *Write It Down. Make It Happen: Knowing What You Want—And Getting It!* (New York: Simon and Schuster, 2001)

Cheryl Richardson, *Take Time for Your Life: A 7-Step Program for Creating the Life You Want* (New York: Random House, 1998)

Eckhart Tolle, *A New Earth: Awakening to Your Life's Purpose* (New York: Penguin Group, 2005)

Eckhart Tolle, *The Power of Now: A Guide to Spiritual Enlightenment* (Navato, CA: New World Library, 1999)

Eckhart Tolle, *Stillness Speaks* (Navato, CA: New World Library, 2003)

Iyanla Vanzant, *One Day My Soul Just Opened Up: 40 Days and 40 Nights Toward Spiritual Strength and Personal Growth* (New York: Simon and Schuster, 1998)

NOTES

Step 2

Page

28   *Saying yes to change*   Joan Borysenko and Gordon Dveirin, *Saying Yes to Change: Essential Wisdom for Your Journey* (Carlsbad, CA: Hay House, Inc., 2006).

36   *Statistics reveal that since 1950*   "This New House," *Mother Jones*, March/April 2005.

38   *According to the Federal Reserve*   Brian K. Bucks, Arthur B. Kennichell, and Kevin B. Moore, "Recent Changes in U.S. Family Finance: Evidence from the 2001 and 2004 Survey of Consumer Finances," *Federal Reserve Bulletin*, vol. 92 (February 2006), A1–A38, http://www.federalreserve.gov/pubs/oss/oss2/2004/bull0206.pdf.

Step 3

Page

56   *Statistics by ACNielsen*   Norman Herr, "Television & Health," in *The Sourcebook for Teaching Science: Strategies, Activities, and Internet Resources* (2001), http://www.csun.edu/~vceed002/health/docs/tv&health.html (accessed January 19, 2007).

61 *According to the Cellular*   Matt Sundeen, "Cell Phones and Highway Safety: 2005 Legislative Update," National Conference of State Legislatures, http://www .ncsl.org/programs/transportation/cellphoneupdate05 .htm (accessed January 19, 2007).

62 *A study in Perth, Australia*   Bob Braun Jr., "Overview: More Phones, More Driving, and More Liability," *Braun Consulting News* 8, no. 1 (Summer 2005), http://www.braunconsulting.com/bcg/newsletters/ summer2005/summer20051.html (accessed January 19, 2007).

66 *according to Robert Kubey*   Norman Herr, "Television & Health," in *The Sourcebook for Teaching Science: Strategies, Activities, and Internet Resources* (2001), http://www.csun.edu/~vceed002/health/docs/ tv&health.html (accessed January 19, 2007).

67 *Television's attraction*   Marie Winn, *The Plug-In Drug: Television, Computers, and Family Life*, 2nd ed. (New York: Penguin Books, 2002).

67 *study conducted at the Hammersmith Hospital*   "Nintendo Neurology," Science and the Citizen, *Scientific American*, August 1998.

Step 4

Page
83 *Our deepest fear*   Marianne Williamson, *A Return to Love: Reflections on the Principles of "A Course in Miracles"* (New York: HarperCollins, 1992).

85   *Resistance is also*   Gregg Levoy, *Callings: Finding and Following an Authentic Life* (New York: Three Rivers Press, 1998).

89   *That which is like*   Esther and Jerry Hicks, *Ask and It Is Given: Learning to Manifest Your Desires* (Carlsbad, CA: Hay House, Inc., 2004).

89   *In order to receive*   Laurence Boldt, *The Tao of Abundance: Eight Ancient Principles for Living Abundantly in the 21st Century* (New York: Penguin Group, 1999).

Step 5

Page

104   *Studies show that*   Shankar Vedantam, "Social Isolation Growing in U.S.," *Washington Post*, June 23, 2006.

104   *Further, psychiatric disorders*   Allan V. Horwitz and Jerome C. Wakefield, "The Age of Depression," *Public Interest*, no. 158 (Winter 2005).

105   *Social isolation*   Scott Allen, "It's Lonely Out There," *Boston Globe*, June 23, 2006, http://www.boston.com/news/nation/articles/2006/06/23/its_lonely_out_there/ (accessed January 19, 2007).

111   *A new cultural*   Mary Pipher, *The Shelter of Each Other: Rebuilding Our Families* (New York: G. P. Putnam's Sons, 1996).

Step 6

Page

128 *The more you live* Eckhart Tolle, *Stillness Speaks* (Navato, CA: New World Library, 2003).

130 *The body* Louise L. Hay, *You Can Heal Your Life* (Carlsbad, CA: Hay House, Inc., 1999).

143 *There's no lack* Ravi Dykema, "This Very Moment Is Magical: An Interview with Dan Millman," *Nexus: Colorado's Holistic Journal*, July/August 2006, https://www.nexuspub.com/articles/2006/interview_dan _millman_junaug2006.htm (accessed January 19, 2007).

Step 7

Page

152 *It is this spiritual freedom* Victor Frankl, *Man's Search for Meaning* (New York: Washington Square Press, 1984).

155 *His unique opportunity* Victor Frankl, *Man's Search for Meaning* (New York: Washington Square Press, 1984).

159 *What he found was* Masaru Emoto, *The Hidden Messages in Water* (Hillsboro, OR: Beyond Words, 2004).

Step 8

Page

188 *Until one is committed* William H. Murray, *The Scottish Himalayan Expedition* (1951), quoted in Meredith

Lee, "Popular Quotes: Commitment," The Goethe Society of North America, http://www.goethesociety .org/pages/quotescom.html (accessed January 19, 2007).

Conclusion

Page

198   *Joy does not come*   Eckhart Tolle, *A New Earth: Awakening to Your Life's Purpose* (New York: Penguin Group, 2005).

To Write to the Author

If you wish to contact the author or would like more information about this book, please write to the author in care of Llewellyn Worldwide and we will forward your request. Both the author and publisher appreciate hearing from you and learning of your enjoyment of this book and how it has helped you. Llewellyn Worldwide cannot guarantee that every letter written to the author can be answered, but all will be forwarded. Please write to:

Karen Mehringer
℅ Llewellyn Worldwide
2143 Wooddale Drive, Dept. 0-7387-1053-9
Woodbury, MN 55125-2989, U.S.A.

Please enclose a self-addressed stamped envelope for reply,
or $1.00 to cover costs. If outside U.S.A., enclose
international postal reply coupon.

Many of Llewellyn's authors have websites with additional information and resources. For more information, please visit our website at:

www.llewellyn.com